Do Justice, Love Kindness, Walk Humbly

The First Hundred Years of Watts Street Baptist Church

1923 to 2023

Rebecca Ragsdale Lallier

ISBN: 978-1-962624-81-7

To the people of Watts Street Baptist Church—past, present, and future

Table of Contents

History is instructive. What it suggests to people is that even if they do little things, if they walk on the picket line, if they join a vigil, if they write a letter to their local newspaper... Anything they do, however small, becomes part of a much larger sort of flow of energy. And when enough people do enough things, however small they are, then change takes place.
--Howard Zinn

History is who we are and why we are the way we are.
--David McCullough

Introduction

One hundred years. How do you possibly summarize the history of a people and a place over that amount of time? It's a daunting proposal. Thankfully for all of us, Becky Lallier didn't let that intimidate her. For the last several years, she has been combing through church records, interviewing people, navigating public events, and behind- the-scenes conversations. She has worked not just on the public facts but also on weaving together many of the deeper truths of this place, beloved to so many of us. Her final product is a delight, and her love for the church comes through it all.

Over the years of her work on this project, I have witnessed Becky come to terms with many of the challenges of being church together, learning about conflicts and feelings and differing interpretations of events. How something is remembered one way in people's stories is often reflected differently in written reports, and how the truth is rarely one or the other. She has grasped the complexities it presents for a group of people together to try and follow God's prompting and how many important things are not ever written down.

Still, I love how she puts it in her conclusion that she has written *a* history of Watts Street, not *the* history of Watts Street. No one could write the full history of the ins and outs of one year in the life of a church, much less one hundred. This history is nevertheless a marvel. It is a joy to read, to imagine that in the same spaces where we gather now, there has been week after week, year after year, generation after generation, including those who first ran the halls as children becoming grandparents to those who do that now.

There has been an awful lot of ink spilled in the last 25 years, wondering about the future of the church in the world. What a gift then to have a thriving congregation that knows its call to live God's love in the world and also that the church itself doesn't equal God to keep things in a healthy perspective. May we always be able to laugh at our foibles, examine our brokenness and flaws, and pray for God's spirit—to inspire us and grow our story alongside God's in the hundred years to come.

Rev. Dorisanne Cooper

October 2023

Having been led, as we believe, by the Spirit of God ... [we] joyfully enter into covenant with one another, as one body in Christ.

—1923 Covenant

Beginnings, 1923 to 1946

On Sunday, January 14, 1923, a group of devoted churchgoers met in the auditorium of Watts School to plan for a new church.

"The meeting was opened with singing 'Blessed be the Tie that Binds.' As this body sang this hymn, it seemed that they were truly bound together with the tie of Christian love," wrote Mrs. J. M. Cheek, the church's first historian.

Watts Street Baptist Church had its origins in the beginnings of what would later become the church. A century later, it thrives still.

The times were propitious. Durham was a bustling place in 1923. Americans had won the Great War, and the devastating flu pandemic of 1918-1920 had passed. Prohibition was the law of the land and women had gained the right to vote, despite North Carolina refusing to ratify the 19th Amendment. The "Roaring Twenties" were underway. The 310 square miles of the county was home to more than 42,000 people. The population of the city of Durham held roughly half of the people—21,719 in 1920, a more than threefold increase from the turn of the century.

The 1923 Hill's Durham City Directory boasted 46 churches, with a white membership of 10,961. It is not clear if the 46 churches included Black churches. Civic organizations abounded, and the city residents enjoyed two parks with swimming pools, tennis courts, and playgrounds. A nine-hole golf course was being built.

The Southern Conservatory of Music, built in 1898 to bring more culture to Durham, occupied an imposing building on the corner of Main and Duke Streets, where young women came to learn piano, voice, cello, violin, and harp. Durham's institutions of higher learning included a business school, Trinity College, and a "National Training School (colored)," as it is listed in the directory.

"Durham is recognized as being one of the leading educational centers of the South," the directory boasted.

The local economy was solidly based on tobacco and textiles, and both industries were flourishing. North Carolina would overtake Massachusetts as the nation's leading producer of textiles in 1923.

And, city leaders reported proudly, the city had 60 miles of sewers. "In the next year or two, it is expected that dry closets will be practically eliminated in the city."

The directory did not mention the thriving black community, Hayti, known as Black Wall Street. In 1920s Durham, the Klan was still a prominent presence. The United Daughters of the Confederacy were lobbying for a statue honoring Confederate veterans. It would be put up in 1924 in front of the county courthouse.

Durham historian Jean Bradley Anderson refers to 1924 as annus mirablis—Durham's year of miracles. The Duke family, wealthy from tobacco, had long been generous to the Durham community, and there were rumors of more to come. In December 1924, James B. Duke announced the creation of the Duke endowment with a gift of $40 million, much of it to enhance Trinity College, renaming it Duke University. The gift would lead to a building and cultural boom.

It was in this atmosphere of possibility and future growth that Watts Street's founders met. They came from other Baptist churches in Durham: First Baptist, West Durham Baptist (now Greystone), and Temple Baptist. It was clear that the area around Trinity College would grow rapidly, and they wanted a Baptist presence in the area.

They moved quickly. They selected a chairman, appointed a secretary, and created a committee of 25 members representing various Baptist churches to assess the need. They met again two weeks later, having already decided to buy lots across from the school on the northeast corner of Watts and Urban for $10,000. A canvas of the neighborhood had turned up 127 likely members. They appointed a committee to draw up a church covenant and rules of order, planned for a Sunday School, and set Sunday, March 4, as the day the church would have its official beginning. They planned to meet at Watts School until they could build their church.

In February, they appointed more committees for correspondence and organization and made more decisions for the kind of church they wanted. They approved leaflets and adopted the six-point plan for use in Sunday School. The six-point plan was adapted from the popular efficiency movement and widely used at the time in Southern Baptist circles. The weekly goal for each student was to reach 100 percent: a student got 20 percent for showing up, with an additional 10 percent if they made it on time; 10 percent for remembering to bring their bible; 20 percent if they stayed for the worship service, and 30 percent more if they came having studied their lesson the night before. Contributing an offering brought an additional 10 percent, leading to a perfect score of 100. The system was applied to children's and adult Sunday School classes.

For their covenant, the founders turned to an old standard that had been used in Baptist churches throughout communities in the North and South for decades and first published in 1853—but they left out a key phrase. They declined to covenant "to abstain from the sale and use of intoxicating drinks as a beverage." It was an unusual move for a Southern Baptist church in 1923.

The edited covenant and rules of order were approved unanimously. They agreed the church would be called Watts Street Baptist Church. Blessings and support came from many members of the area's other Baptist churches and the Mount Zion Baptist Association.

As planned, they began formally at 3 PM ON Sunday, March 4, at Watts School. There were six ministers there, forming a presbytery and led by the Rev. T.M. Green of West Durham Baptist Church. Green gave the call, and 126 people came forward with their letters, releasing them from their current churches to form the new Watts Street Baptist Church (WSBC). In a solemn moment, they all stood and pledged themselves to their new church's covenant. (The deacons decided later that all those who submitted a letter by March 17 would be considered charter members, giving a total of 157.) "Dr. J. W. Lynch then delivered to those present words of great hope and encouragement and advice that will long be remembered," the deacons' minutes record, without including his comments.

Eight deacons were nominated, and four of them were ordained on the spot, the other four having already been ordained. Three trustees were selected, and a Sunday School superintendent and a church clerk were appointed. A Relief Committee was appointed to see who among the new congregation might need help.

# # #

The new congregation looked to build a church building in an optimistic moment in time.

"With our increased wealth, with our diffusion of architectural taste, and, above all, with our enlightened appreciation of religion as a prime factor in our civilization, is it too much to expect that our churches will more and more in their buildings seek beauty and impressiveness, as well as practical utility?" asked P.E. Burroughs in his book, *A Complete Guide to Church Building,* published by the Sunday School Board of the Southern Baptist Convention in 1923.

Churches in the United States began as meeting houses designed for preaching and worship services. With the arrival of the Sunday School movement, stressing Christian education, churches had become places of worship and education, and their buildings expanded. Now, Burroughs wrote, it was time to add the social element. Young people were expanding their horizons in ways their elders did not always consider appropriate. The church needed to offer a social option to all its members. To do this, churches now needed kitchens, he wrote, adding that it would soon be as unthinkable to build a church without a kitchen as it was now unthinkable to build a hotel without a kitchen.

The new congregation turned to Stanhope Johnson, a Lynchburg architect, for a design. The church was to look different from many Baptist churches and was built in a Gothic style that matched the new campus being built nearby. The church would be a beautiful stone-faced building, the sanctuary being full of light, with soaring arches and stained-glass windows. The new church included a bell tower but no steeple. The largest stained-glass window facing the street was to be of Jesus, the Good Shepherd.

Progress towards building and organizing continued at a rapid pace that spring and summer, and on September 7, 1923, the first called pastor, Rev. Howard L. Weeks, gave his first sermon to his new congregation.

# # #

This collage of Weeks, the new church, Watts School where the church first met, his home (presumably), and the Nash automobile he was so proud of ran in the local newspaper when Weeks was introduced to the Durham community.

Weeks was a veteran pastor.

"Howard Weeks is described as gruff, outspoken, a minister who expected to have a major voice in everything the church did. He was very forceful, in and out of the pulpit. Weeks was a stocky man who did not hesitate to voice his opinion, sometimes quite bluntly," an earlier history recorded.

His tenure would be short.

A native of Missouri and an 1899 graduate of Southern Baptist Seminary in Louisville, he had held pastorates in Missouri, Mississippi, Ohio, and South Carolina. He was credited with leading successful building programs. He came to Watts Street from Abbeville, South Carolina, where he had served for two years.

He "comes to Durham with the reputation of being one of the biggest men in the Baptist denomination. He is an excellent speaker and a man with a pleasing personality," the Durham Morning Herald announced. "He is expected to make an excellent addition to the ministerial forces of the city." Weeks, who also had an eye for business opportunities, took advantage of his newspaper introduction to include an endorsement of his Nash automobile.

When Weeks arrived, the congregation was still meeting at Watts school. The first job was to build a church.

John T. Salmon, chair of Watts Street's building committee, was a prominent builder himself and chair of the building committee. He and C. H. Shipp, another Watts Street member, owned Consolidated Construction, the company hired to build the new church. They had already built several churches in Durham, including First Baptist, Trinity Methodist, Temple Baptist, and Grace Baptist. He had also built several edifices on college campuses throughout the state, including the East Duke building at nearby Trinity College. Salmon was a leader in the Durham community, serving for many years on the city council.

Perhaps inevitably, Salmon and Weeks clashed. The surviving records leave us with no details but plenty of references to the ongoing conflict. Weeks may have wanted a less expensive building, while Salmon wanted a church he could be especially proud of as a church member and as a builder. Weeks apparently wanted the standard brick, while Salmon was determined on the beautiful stone facings that adorn the church today.

The first service in the new building was held at 3 PM on April 5, 1925. The day "stands out as one of the mountain peaks in the experience of the Church. The doors of our church building were thrown open, and for the first time, we worshipped in our own house," Mrs. Cheek recorded. "Truly we felt we could say with the Psalmist 'I was glad when they said unto me let us go into the house of the Lord.'"

The service received wide press coverage, and many of the city's pastors attended. Spring was revival season, and an earlier history says Weeks hosted two very successful revivals at Watts Street in 1925.

But all was not well with Weeks and the church. The feud between Salmon and Weeks had spilled over to the congregation, and by the summer, the deacons began pressuring Weeks to resign. He was not receptive to the idea. When a committee of deacons approached him to formally ask him for his resignation, he suggested the deacons go home and pray for themselves and the church. A second formal "suggestion" was made, only to be curtly rejected.

The deacons were apparently frustrated not only with their conflicts within the church but with Weeks's activities outside of it. His son, H. Raymond Weeks, an Atlanta architect, had moved to Durham, and he and his father started building houses. With the Duke endowment boosting all kinds of activity in Durham, it was a good time to be investing in Durham properties. The deacons apparently thought the church should receive Weeks's full attention.

On November 6, Weeks brought the conflict before the congregation in the Sunday morning service, asking for a vote of confidence. Weeks asked that all in favor of him staying stand. He stood on one side of the pulpit, and his son stood on the other for ease of counting. About 25 people stood up. Then he asked that all who thought he should leave please stand up. Less than a dozen people stood. Roughly 150 people chose not to vote, and Weeks interpreted this as his vote of confidence.

Weeks apparently took his complaints to the newspaper. "The minister declared that he had not been receiving the proper support from the church members and stated that his work here would not be a success unless they cooperated with him more earnestly," the newspaper duly reported. Unnamed church officials denied rumors that Weeks had resigned, saying that Weeks had only asked for more support and that members of the congregation unanimously voted him that.

The deacons struck back, calling a churchwide meeting for the next week. When Weeks questioned their right to call such a meeting and again refused to resign, the deacons went on with their meeting and passed a motion declaring the pulpit vacant. Weeks, finally seeing the handwriting on the wall, asked to resign, and the motion declaring the pulpit empty was rescinded, and his resignation was accepted, effective immediately.

The Durham paper dutifully reported Weeks's resignation and quoted, again, unnamed church officials, insisting that there had been no friction and that no one had ever asked for Weeks's resignation.

"I wish to say merely that whatever sense of injustice or cruel wrong I may feel now, I prefer to bear it in silence," Weeks told the paper. Then he went on to say that he enjoyed much support from his congregation and that the publicity the situation received was not his fault. "My life has been an open book. Those who are actually responsible for the unfortunate condition in the Watts Street church are also known to many in our city."

Under Weeks's leadership, however tempestuous, important things were accomplished. The church was constructed and opened its doors, and membership climbed from 157 to 237. A strong Sunday School program was organized, especially for the younger age groups.

Weeks lingered in Durham for a few months and eventually accepted a call to Bluefield, West Virginia, where his blunt personality was perhaps better appreciated. He served there for 12 years, retiring in 1938. He moved to Chapel Hill in retirement and served as a "supply" or interim pastor for several years. His son, Raymond, remained in Durham and built a successful career as an architect. He and his family left Watts Street when his father did and joined First Baptist.

But the harsh feelings between the church and its first pastor seemed to dissipate over the years.

The Raymond Weeks family returned as members of Watts Street in 1953. In August 1956, Warren Carr, then Watts Street's pastor, shared the officiating duties with Rev. Weeks for the wedding of Weeks's granddaughter at her parents' home in Durham. Two months later, Raymond, 56, died suddenly of a heart attack and his funeral was held at Watts Street.

In March 1958, Weeks and his wife were back at Watts Street for its 35th anniversary celebration. Weeks read the scripture lesson for the service, stood in a receiving line, and saw his photograph, along with other former pastors, hung in the hall leading to the pastor's study.

Weeks died eight months later. His obituary in Durham identified him prominently as Watts Street's first pastor.

# # #

Announcement of the Rev. C. S. Green's arrival.

Among the 25 people standing in support of Rev. Weeks at the contentious November 6 church service was a young man who would become the new pastor and lead the church for seven years.

Charles Sylvester Green had impeccable Baptist credentials. He was the son of Rev. T. M. Green, former pastor of West Durham Baptist (now Greystone), who had been a prime mover in the effort to create Watts Street. The elder Green left West Durham to work with the Mount Zion Baptist Association. In that role, he had listened to many complaints from Weeks, deacons, and church members about the situation at Watts Street, telling his son of his frustrations and his feeling that everyone involved could have been kinder.

The younger Green, with his eye on a teaching career, had graduated from Wake Forest College, a Baptist College in the throes of the debate over evolution when Green had been a student there. Wake Forest's position was decidedly moderate, but the debate occupied North Carolina Baptists and much of the country for decades. In some circles, it still does.

In addition to his father, Green's family included his father's cousin, B. W. Spilman, who became known as "Mr. Sunday School" for the many years he spent working for a uniform education and curriculum for Baptists. His work was part of a much larger, nondenominational movement for Christian education. Spillman would go on to found Ridgecrest, a Baptist retreat in the North Carolina mountains.

In 1925, Sylvester Green was teaching English at Durham High School and serving as president of the Baptist Young People's Union, traveling the state and building programs. Green also worked for the Durham newspapers, covering mostly religious topics. He was also a graduate student at Duke, working on a PhD in English, hoping to teach in college.

Green was described as "energetic beyond belief." He would work hard and long for Watts Street Church.

Reading the spirited autobiography Green left us, one gets the sense of an educated, modern man always in motion, a friendly, kind young man who always had places to go and people to see. He noted with pride that his co-workers at the Herald did not consider him "stuck up," as many college boys were perceived to be. He preached a faith of reason and knowledge. He was not a fan of emotionally overwrought revivals. His vision, as suited a teacher, was of an educated laity caring for each other and all of God's people.

Green had already proved his organizing and leadership abilities to the deacons. When Dr. Norris, one of the deacons, suggested that "something should be done to corral the interest of the men of the church in the work of the church," Green started monthly dinners, which were deemed a great success. When Weeks departed, Green took on the job of finding a preacher for each Sunday morning, sometimes filling in himself.

Finding a new pastor would not be easy. By the time the deacons began to consider if their new pastor had been sitting in the congregation all along, two prospects had already declined an offer, perhaps put off by the experience of Watts Street's first pastor.

After 11 PM on the night of January 17, 1926, the deacons paid a call. Green wrote that he answered the door at his mother's home and found all eight deacons standing on the porch. "I asked them in; our front room was still comfortable, although I had already banked the furnace fire for the night." The group stayed for hours, hoping to convince Green to become their pastor. Green expressed his concern about how the church had treated Weeks. He finally agreed to consider their offer, setting two conditions: no one would mention the Weeks affair to him, and the deacons would not pressure him.

By the end of February, Green was ready to accept. Ministers speak of having their call to the ministry—a moment of spiritual clarity when they know what God wants of them. Green was concerned as to whether he had such a call. He decided that the deacons all calling him, with no urging on his part, would qualify. He was concerned about his lack of formal training and planned to get a divinity degree at Duke as expeditiously as possible. (He earned a Duke divinity degree in 1930, but he would write later that a degree from Duke impressed no one in Baptist circles. For many decades, a degree from Southern Seminary in Louisville, Kentucky, was the only degree that counted.)

He planned to finish out his year of teaching. The church ordained him on May 30, 1926, in a well-attended ceremony in the new sanctuary. Mr. Sunday School showed up to preach the sermon, and the newspaper article, perhaps written by Green, led off with the statement that Green's ordination had been his father's deepest wish. And then, as if accepting a call to the ministry was not enough to change, Green invited the congregation to a "special ceremony" at the church the next week. About 150 people showed up and learned that the "special ceremony" was his wedding to Mary Morris.

For all his education, energy, and hard work, Green was still a young man thrust into his father's world. The elder Green had died suddenly in January 1925. As Sylvester took his place among his father's colleagues, there was talk about his youth and inexperience.

He set to work with his usual level of energy. With no staff to help, he sent out cards to church members weekly, published bulletins, hosted revivals, and worked in all aspects of the church. His salary was $3,300 a year, with no expenses for anything. Always an educator, by his second year, he was giving Sunday School teachers an exam with ten essay questions about teaching, home study, and the purpose of Sunday School. Teachers were to sign a pledge and turn it into Green.

Other features of Watts Street during Green's time were a sunrise Thanksgiving service at 7 AM, annual church picnics at various city parks, and an elaborate reception each year to celebrate the anniversary of the founding of Watts Street. Green often wrote sketches about the church and its past and future for these regular gatherings. The 1929 invitation reads: "There will be mirth-provoking stunts; novelty musical numbers; selected readings; and varied instrumental music, piano, violin, and orchestra. The grand finale of the evening will be the group singing with the aid of illustrated song slides displayed by the stereopticon."

Services with Green ran for one hour exactly. He preached from notes, without writing it all out beforehand, always keeping the sermon to exactly twenty minutes. He loved to keep track of his activities. In 1927, he recorded 74 sermons, 135 additional talks, 1168 pastoral calls, 18 funerals, 10 marriages, 13 baptisms, and 4 observances of the Lord's Supper. The church gained 77 new members, 59 by letter, 5 by statement, and 13 by baptism. "I always enjoyed compiling statistics. I am sure no one was half so impressed as I was myself," Green wrote. When his daughter was born in 1931, Green made use of his time at the hospital. "During the final moments, and while Mary was in the delivery room, I went around the hospital visiting patients."

In all his vigorous endeavors, Watts Street's first Daily Vacation Bible School is the only thing he ever reported as taxing his energy. The first DVBSs were held in 1924; Watts Street's first was held in 1928. The average daily attendance was 245, and a group photo, now in the church library, ran in the newspaper. Green was particularly proud that the school was open to the larger Durham community (at least the white community). Children from the Wright's Refuge for Children attended every day, something that Green said was "one of the finest things of the school."

Registration came with what must have been a special attraction in 1928. "When we enroll them, we will give them a free automobile ride," Green boasted.

The school began with a parade around the Trinity Park neighborhood and closed two weeks later with much ceremony on Friday evening, June 15. More than 200 children walked into the crowded sanctuary, bearing the United States flag, the Christian flag, and the bible. All the children sang "America," "Onward Christian Soldiers," and "What a Friend We Have in Jesus" before parents and guests visited the individual classrooms to admire the children's work.

"It was a two-weeks affair, and I have to confess that after that two weeks of actual work, plus all the weeks of preparation, I was completely exhausted," Green recalled. "In fact, as I recall, I had to spend several days in bed resting."

DVBS never reached this peak attendance again. By the next year, more churches were hosting their own schools. And two years later, in the Great Depression, the church stopped hosting bible school, not resuming it until the 1940s.

The extensive coverage Watts Street's DVBS received was typical. "Watts Street got good newspaper coverage during all the years of my pastorate. The papers were not only willing to print whatever I wrote and brought in, but they were constantly asking me for coverage of events to which I was in any way related. That was a marked asset in my work." Green also reported on Baptist conventions and denominational meetings for Baptist publications and the wire services.

Green felt strongly about communication within the church, too, and with no support staff or funds, he published a church directory. He believed that the growth of the church required a publication of its own. The deacons were not interested, but Green went ahead and published a church newsletter.

"I am sure it did a lot of good. But I was never happy about the lack of enthusiasm on the part of the Deacons," Green wrote. At the downtown post office, he found in the trash bin "38 envelopes I had laboriously addressed to as many families of the church." He wrote that he never mentioned his discovery. "I reasoned, What's the use? In a few months, the publication was discontinued, and to this day, not a single member of that Board has ever mentioned missing it and wondering what happened."

# # #

The deacons were the governing body of the church, and its minutes from these years show a Baptist church very much a part of the larger Baptist community. Donations went regularly to the NC Baptist Orphanage, the Wright's Refuge, and the King's Daughter's Home. The church held services at the county home and in prison. Watts Street women were active in many kinds of outreach. Messengers went annually to the Mount Zion Baptist Association, the North Carolina Baptist Association, and the Southern Baptist Association, and Green attended the Baptist World Alliance in Toronto in 1928.

The congregation was growing, and the deacons increased their numbers from eight to twelve. They met in the ladies' parlor at church or in each other's homes, and many meetings included a meal. Deacon minutes show repeated concern about lack of money and lack of motivation from church members. The deacons often wanted more emphasis on midweek worship and more ministry to Duke students.

In 1926, the deacons voted women could serve on the finance committee, but they left us no hint as to who or why. On June 9, they refused to issue the letters necessary to let Annie May and Elizabeth Hutchins move their membership to Temple Baptist Church at the request of their father, Brother A. N. Hutchins. They left us no details on the family drama involved. The deacons "erased" Mrs. Holland Holton from the church roll without issuing her a letter. She apparently earned erasure for becoming a Methodist and joining Duke Memorial Methodist Church. Another woman was erased for similar reasons, in her case, moving to a church where her children attended.

In 1928, there was a crisis of "discipline" in the Baptist Young People's Union (BYPU), and the deacons appointed a committee "to take the matter in charge." Apparently, the committee was unsuccessful, and the crisis in programs for young people had spread to the Sunday School because by the fall, the Sunday School superintendent resigned, and a churchwide meeting was called to discuss the crisis. The minutes give us no hint as to the problem or its eventual solution.

At one meeting, the deacons struck a member off their roll because they learned he had never been baptized. At another meeting, they discussed a member who was an "admitted defaulter" at the local post office. Just to make sure their position was clear, they passed a resolution saying the deacon board was "utterly opposed to any violations of law." The offender attended the next meeting, and the deacons voted to forgive him.

The missions of the church seem to have been left largely to the women. From the beginning, Watts Street had an active Women's Missionary Union (WMU). In June of 1928, a newspaper article reported that the Watts Street group received an "efficiency banner" for the good work they did. Green's sermon was titled "Help Those Women," and the scripture was the Mary and Martha story. The local group was one of only nine Southern Baptist Convention

(SBC) churches in the state to earn a banner.

In 1931, a "lack of understanding" was discovered between the Women's Missionary Union and the board of deacons, apparently over how the monies the women raised were to be spent. The deacons— some of them no doubt intimately related to the members of the WMU—appointed a committee of three "to see all the leaders of the WMU and obtain an understanding." Apparently, an understanding was reached because the next meeting minutes report that the treasurer "would make such records and credits as would be pleasing to them," and the women agreed to conform to the policy next year of making gifts to the church as a whole and not, presumably, individual projects. In Baptist churches, the WMU retained its independence for decades, and conflict with male church leaders over how the monies the women raised were to be spent was not uncommon.

The young church struggled with its financial obligations, as most new churches do. WSBC had borrowed more than $30,000 to begin building and then borrowed $80,000 more from Jefferson Standard Life Insurance Company to finish building the church. The money was lent at 7 percent, and the church was to keep up with the interest and pay $8,000 a year for ten years on the principal.

Members pledged support to meet the debt. The Women's Bible Class showed its dedication by pledging to pay $1,000 towards construction. They earned their pledge dollar by hard-earned dollar, selling baked goods and Brunswick stew. All the women in the church solicited money for the building and made a quilt covered in the names of donors.

But by September 1926, the $30,000 loan was due, and the church could not pay it. Pastor Green and H. Clyde Barbee, a local banker, made a plan. They decided that A. J. Draughon (known as Major), W.C. Lyon, C. T. Council, Dr. Carl P. Norris, and J. T. Salmon could afford to help. Major Draughon invited them all to his home, where Green and Barbee explained their plan. They said they thought with a new campaign, they could probably raise about $10,000 more towards the debt. They were asking those gathered there to be responsible for the rest. All five men, including several who had to borrow the money, pledged $4,000 each. In a story that has come down in church lore, Draughon served his guests ice cream after their pledges, saying it was the most expensive ice cream he had ever served.[1]

The Herald reported that Barbee made a surprise announcement to the congregation on the last Sunday in September, saying that a campaign had begun 10 days earlier and the debt would be paid, thanks to the generosity of the congregation and a $5,000 gift from B.N. Duke. At the Sunday morning service on October 3, Professor James Cannon III of Duke addressed the congregation, congratulating them on meeting their obligations and building a temple to God. Council, chair of the finance committee, then struck a match and set fire to a paper representing the debt. Green talked about plans for the church's continued work, and all stood to pledge their support to this new beginning.

The larger debt of $80,000 to the Jefferson Insurance Company remained, and a few years later, the church would find itself unable to keep up with the $8,000 annual payment. But, for the fall, the congregation rejoiced.

The spirit of celebration carried over to a revival at Watts Street the next month. "Three services of unusual spiritual power and strength Sunday marked the close of the special evangelistic services at the Watts Street Baptist Church, which began November 1 and continued through last evening," the Herald reported on November 14, 1926, noting that the church gained 22 new members and 74 people made public professions of faith. The rededications and reconsecrations were "a great good to the entire membership."

Revivals were a regular part of church life for many decades.

---

[1] For many years, when issuing the invitation to join the church, Mel Wiliams would say folks could join by transfer of letter from another church, and if the potential member's church had burned down, they would take the member's word for it and accept them anyway. This addition comes from Major Draughon's experience. His church in Sampson County had burned down and he was unable to produce a letter. The story that has come down in church history is that the founding members did not want to admit Draughon to membership without a letter. The conflict did not last long. Records show Draughon became a member in November 1923, just six months after the church officially began.

Often, churches would come together to hold citywide revivals. Other times, individual churches would hold their own revival. Often, there would be two in a year, in the spring and the fall. Individual preachers became known as great evangelists and would travel the country, hosting revivals. For its first three decades, Watts Street held or took part in revivals regularly.

In the fall of 1929, the United States plunged into the Great Depression. On Monday, October 27, the stock market lost 13 percent of its value. The next day, Black Tuesday, it lost 12 percent more. It would continue to decline through the summer of 1932, losing overall almost 90 percent of its value. The impact on individuals, families, and institutions is hard to overstate. No one knew how long the economic crisis would last.

But Watts Street's troubles predated the big crash. The deacons' minutes chronicle 1929 meetings in May and the Sunday before Black Tuesday when they met to discuss their financial crisis. The deacons appointed a committee to go talk to Jefferson Standards Life Insurance Company. Green, H. C. Barbee, and D. C. May made the trip to Greensboro to meet with company officials, stopping to pray along the way at an outdoor table at a church yard in Elon. May, known for his fervent prayers, prayed long and hard. In Greensboro, they met kindness and sympathy and were asked only to keep up the interest payments on the loan to avoid foreclosure.

They drove back to Durham, rejoicing, little imagining how much worse things would become.

The following November, the deacons, the trustees, and the finance committee met together for "a very frank talk by the pastor" and to pledge to give themselves financially and personally more to the church. A newspaper article reports a contribution of $12,500 at the end of the year to clear the church's debt.

The deacons were about to learn about the young pastor they had chosen. Doubtless, they had hoped for a more compliant man after the experience with Weeks. Certainly, Green proved much easier to get along with, but he lacked neither courage nor determination.

For Green, the Depression was a time to step out in faith. For the church deacons, it was a time to retrench. The church's Finance Committee and deacons "were all fearful of what 1931 might bring, and they preached their pessimism so much it seeped over into the total work of the church." Green wanted to continue the "total work" of the church and told the deacons frankly, "that in my opinion, their faith was slipping … I refused to believe we could not go on."

The popular Daily Vacation Bible School was canceled. Norman Matthews, choir director and organist, was told he could no longer pay singers and that there might be months when his salary was not available. "That was cruel treatment, let's face it! And it was not necessary!" Green wrote.

Green was also told that there was no money for a revival, and he held one anyway. He preached himself—instead of hiring a preacher—and paid the musicians out of the loose offering.

In December of 1931, with the economic situation looking no better, Green wrote that he laid out a plan to carry the church through 1932 and told the deacons he preferred that they declare the church dead rather than more years of this slow, agonizing death. He told them he would have no complaint with whatever they did with his salary and left the meeting to visit the sick.

The finance committee and the deacons voted to almost halve his salary from $4,200 to $2,400. "I feared later I had overstated my case," Green wrote.

"I confess to all kinds of confused emotions following the slash in salary and the general hard times at the church…and that if my leadership had been what it should have been, it would have been avoided."

The next month, Durham leader John Sprunt Hill hosted a breakfast at the Hotel Washington Duke for all the ministers in town and asked them to reassure their congregations that the local banks would not fail. Green was not convinced, but he dutifully informed his congregation of Hill's message.

Two weeks later, Green went to First National Bank to deposit his paycheck from the church and several other checks. It was a tense scene, he reported, and "the directors of the bank were there in full force, including a couple of members of Watts Street, each with a white carnation in his buttonhole." When Green presented his deposit slip, the teller whispered, "Are you sure you want to make this deposit?" Green came to wish he had cashed the check instead when the bank did not open the next morning.

The Durham Sun wrote that the bank's closing was caused by senseless fear and called it "one of the major financial tragedies in the history of Durham."

Green's many other jobs helped keep his family solvent during these difficult years. He wrote, edited, and laid out the church section of the Durham Morning Herald. He continued his many jobs for the larger Baptist organization. He wrote editorials—four a day—for the Herald and the Sun. That assignment grew into his "sermon editorials," which ran in the Herald until late in 1967. With all his freelancing, he was making more than the church had ever paid him and still worked full-time as a minister.

In November 1932, Watts Street would send another group to meet with Jefferson officials. They could not meet the interest on the debt. Barbee would make the trip again, this time joined by J. T. Salmon. The pastor with them would not be Green. Again, they would meet with mercy.

After six years as Watts Street's pastor, Green was ready to move on. He hoped "there would be opened for me an opportunity where I would be able to carry out some of my hopes and plans for church growth without the severe stringency I was experiencing at Watts Street … I had come to the feeling that perhaps my leadership was becoming less effective and that some one else, perhaps with more training in the ministry, might more successfully carry on the work of the church," he wrote.

The church's anniversary celebration in 1932 was the smallest ever, Green reported. Only 140 attended. It was subdued, with the pastor ready to leave and the deacons encouraging him to go. The future of this nine-year-old church was far from clear.

The next month, Green accepted a call from Grove Avenue

Baptist Church in Richmond. Green, as usual, stayed busy until the last minute. As his colleagues gave him a farewell lunch at the Hotel Washington Duke, Green said several asked him to keep an eye out for opportunities for them, too. On their last night in Durham, the Greens attended another going away dinner, and then Green worked until 4 AM finishing an indexing job. The family left for Richmond at 7 AM.

# # #

For all the stories and opinions Green left us, it is still challenging to figure out where he stood on race. There are hints that he was far ahead of many of his contemporaries.

He recorded proudly in his autobiography that when he became pastor at Watts Street, a Jewish girl in his class said she would go and hear him preach because in all the years he had been her teacher, she had never heard him make an "uncomplimentary ethnic reference." That was not by chance, he wrote. He did not think ethnic references were appropriate and believed that they were usually false.

At an evening church service in February 1927 (February was often the occasion of some sort of "Brotherhood" effort), Green preached a sermon on "Lincoln, Our Great Martyred President."

Each year, he did programs at North Carolina College for Negroes (now North Carolina Central University or NCCU). In 1930, he proudly attended White Rock Baptist Church in Durham—at the invitation of its pastor, Dr. Fisher—to hear the Reverend C. S. Morris, a famous preacher from Chicago. His earlier work with the BYPU had included work with leaders at the future NCCU.

In *Our Separate Ways: Women and the Black Freedom Movement in Durham, North Carolina* (UNC Press, 2005), author Christina Green writes that Watts Street was known as a liberal church in the 1930s and quotes a young woman who recalled attended an interracial meeting at Watts Street in the 1930s. It does not seem at all out of the realm of possibility that Rev. Green, in his work with college students, hosted interracial meetings. He writes of women doing most all the mission work: Professor Green writes about groups of Black and

White churchwomen who met across the color line. Were Watts Street women among them? One yearns to know more.

From Grove Avenue, Green became president of Coker College in South Carolina. In 1943, he returned to Durham as editor of the *Herald* and rejoined Watts Street. He continued his support of NCCU. His papers mention donating his library and endowing a scholarship. He carried on a correspondence with Dr. James Sheppard, president at Central. His editorials supported education and put him in a moderate camp on race relations.

The peripatetic pastor would go on to more jobs involving colleges and hospitals, eventually dying in 1980 in Statesville, North Carolina, where he had moved to be with his son. He is buried in Durham. Watts Street pastor Bob McClernon officiated at his funeral.

The Sanctuary as it looked in the church's early years.

# # #

Reverend J. T. Riddick

Watts Street's next pastor, the Rev. J. T. Riddick, hit town like an Old Testament prophet. His message was harsh. God's judgment was upon us because "we have scrapped the Ten Commandments and junked the Sermon on the Mount; we have turned the Lord's day into a deadly frolic on our highways and turned to the funny paper and jazz music for our social past-time," he thundered.

He was a known quantity, having been the pastor at Temple Baptist Church in Durham from 1912 to 1917. He wore a black frock coat— a style more popular in the previous century—and preached the gospel with an evangelical fervor. Several longtime members remember being a little afraid of him when they were children.

While he was at Temple Baptist Church, he had increased the membership from 500 to 800, and Watts Street Deacons hoped he would do the same for them. Under his leadership, Temple set up a committee to police members' behavior, with a focus on alcohol. "Large congregations gathered Sunday after Sunday to hear his fearless messages on evil conditions in Durham," Temple's church history records.

His message at Watts Street would be similar.

When he returned to Durham from Norfolk, Virginia, in 1932, the Depression was still worsening, but Riddick was sure he had the answer.

"Our sure return to prosperity as a nation lies more surely in our return to God and His law of right living than to any other thing that we can bring to bear on society and business," Riddick preached. "Victory is ours in the name of the Lord God of hosts.

"I say this despite the fact that our country is on the verge of plunging back into the throes of the damnable saloon by the will of the politicians of America. I say this despite the fact that many church members and Christians are favoring the repeal of the greatest moral law ever passed by congress."

He was not happy about the pending repeal of Prohibition. One wonders if he had noticed what was missing from the Watts Street covenant.

Riddick was a popular evangelist for the Southern Baptist Convention, and it was estimated that he had preached 270 revivals in his career. He was also among the new generation of radio preachers. By 1930, more than half of American homes had a radio, and preachers were learning to take advantage of the new technology to reach people. Every Thursday, on local station WDNC, Riddick would give his spiritual fireside chats.

He was a North Carolina native and attended Southern Baptist Theological Seminary in Louisville, Kentucky. He started Watts Street's library by offering to donate 100 volumes from his personal library, known to be one of the largest in the state. He served on the SBC's Home Missions Board and was a trustee at Campbell College. On wintery Saturday nights, he would visit the church to start a fire in the furnace and bank it so the congregation would find a warm and welcoming church the next morning.

He preached about saving the home. "If we put as much of the time and attention on our homes as we are putting on other things … we would have much less youth lawlessness and maiden moral inconsistencies: fewer criminals and fewer people needing 'handouts.'"

Riddick saw a battle ahead for the country and for the churches' survival, and he plunged into the fray. In his first meeting with the deacons, he outlined how to help the church. "He recommended strongly that we should practice personal visitation, that our prayer life should be given much attention, that we should be helpful to each other, and that we should pay our pledges religiously."

The financial stress, never absent, was heightened in these dark years of poverty. The deacons agreed to keep the church open at all hours, hoping to offer a refuge for prayer in a troubled world.

In September 1933, the deacons discovered that the church budget was $572.15 short. They passed the hat in their meeting and, collected $235, and instructed Riddick and D. C. Barbee to "see individual members for the balance."

Their hard work and Riddick's fiery preaching began to show results. In January 1934, the deacons authorized a $300 love offering to Riddick. The next month they established a bell system for Sunday School and approved money to buy hymnals. In April, they adjourned their meeting so they could attend a revival meeting led by Gipsey Smith, a Romani evangelist who had been invited by the Durham Ministerial Association to stir Durham souls.

But the same problems remained with the membership and money. In March, they made a list of members who did not attend or contribute financially. In May, they planned personal visits to the recalcitrant. In November, they created an inactive list, perhaps giving in to reality. One of these recalcitrant members actually attended a deacon meeting and explained his case. The Rev. L. B. Boney, a retired pastor, explained that he had too little money to contribute and did not attend regularly because of his work, filling in for other pastors. The deacons told him they understood.

Each year, meeting the interest on the loan raised challenges, and it seems they often had a separate committee to raise the funds. In 1934, the amount due was $1,280, and the deacons thanked J. L. Wilkerson and his co-workers for raising it.

The next year, C. T. Council, one of the founders of the popular BC powders, donated $42,000 to the church to pay off the loan with Jefferson. Henceforth, Watts Street would be mortgage-free. Six months later, the deacons approved a motion to dedicate a large front window to Mr. C. T. Council as a memorial to his family "in appreciation of his large gift making possible the payment in full of all mortgage and loan against the church."

The congregation rejoiced.

The check that paid Watts Street's mortgage in 1935.

The deacons' notes continue to report on standard things: the Boy Scouts continue what seems to be a regular search for a sponsor, and a men's Sunday School class agrees to take on the job. There is a mention—just a mention—of a Watts Street Girl Scout troop, its members running through the church halls.

The pastor's office was moved to the third floor. Singers were hired for the choir. In the summer, members joined with members from First Baptist and made a visit to the Thomasville orphanage and decided to give each month's first Sunday loose offering to the orphanage. They discussed their regular Thanksgiving service and approved a sign for outside the church. They planned a stewardship revival and decided to hold quarterly business meetings, presumably for the whole church.

Riddick died on December 20, 1938, at his home. His death was "not altogether unexpected," the newspaper reported, saying that Riddick had an earlier heart attack. A funeral service was held at Watts Street, and his burial was in Norfolk, Virginia, where he had spent a large part of his career.

Tributes poured in. "Of all the body of ministers who look after the spiritual interests of the people of this city, no man is held in greater esteem by men and women of various denominations," the paper declared. The Women's Missionary Society said Riddick "left the world better than he found it because of so many rescued souls."

The deacons voted to pay Mrs. Riddick's bills for 13 months and purchase a bronze plate for a window in memory of him.

# # #

The church called Owen Herring, an educated, sensitive man who left the fire and brimstone behind, for its next pastor. His successor, Warren Carr, would call Herring a "good, decent, gentle man" who gathered "the people not around himself, but around the Christ." Herring's soothing ways and peaceful manner made for a congregation where "There was no need to heal brokenness, to patch up the wounds, division, to harmonize discordance," Carr wrote.

He arrived in June 1939 with his wife, Ethel, and two young children. Two more children would be born to the Herring family during their years at Watts Street. One longtime member remembers Herring interrupting his sermon to admonish his offspring to better behavior during the service.

The Reverend Owen Herring

Herring graduated from Wake Forest College in 1913, then earned master's and doctorate degrees in theology from Southern Seminary in Louisville, and then added a doctorate in divinity from Georgetown College in Kentucky. He came to Watts Street from Winchester, Kentucky.

The church welcomed the Herrings with a reception on June 16, 1939. Six weeks later, Hitler invaded Poland. The repercussions would be felt throughout much of the world for the next six years and would darken Herring's years at Watts Street.

Before Pearl Harbor Sunday shattered Americans' sense of isolation from the war, Durham, like many other places, had already begun to experience the buildup to World War II. Private efforts were underway to help populations in Hitler's path, and the nation's first peacetime draft was established in September of 1940. Thousands of Durham men registered and two army contingents, one black and one white, left for training at Fort Bragg. National Guard units were called up and Fort Bragg was expanded and turned into one of the largest army installations in the nation, providing work for Durham's skilled workers.

In 1942, over vociferous protests from the 1,325 families that would lose their homes and valuable farmland, Camp Butner was built in six months just 12 miles from Durham. Workers and merchants benefited. The camp would train more than 30,000 soldiers on its 40,000 acres and serve as a POW camp and military hospital. A bus ran from the camp to Durham, and soldiers off duty changed life for city residents. Soldiers were everywhere in town, crowding movie theaters, ice cream parlors, the skating rink, and whatever else they could find. Joints and clubs of all kinds sprang up to serve the soldiers. Hayti gained a reputation as a particularly wild locale, and military police patrolled there regularly.

Church leaders expressed concern about drunkenness and prostitution stemming from this sudden increase in population. Watts Street members, led by the example of the Herrings, opened their church and their homes to soldiers. The Red Cross set up a sewing room in Watts Street, open to volunteers of all religions. Volunteers knitted, sewed, and made surgical dressings.

As the war continued, blackouts and air-raid drills became common practice. Sirens were placed on buildings and tested weekly. Newspapers announced, perhaps hoping to reassure residents, that Durham had purchased the most powerful siren made and announced the dates for blackout practices. The sirens and the weekly tests continued through the cold war with Russia.

Throughout the fear and terror, Ethel Herring sought to help soldiers, students, and young people facing an uncertain future. She had worked in organizing youth groups in Kentucky before her marriage. In Durham, she organized educational and social programs for young men and women and made a special effort to reach Duke students.

A current Watts Street member, Greer Clayton, remembers how Ethel Herring influenced Clayton after her time at Watts Street. Clayton, from South Carolina, was at Fort Caswell with her parents for a week-long event for Training Union leaders in the late 1950s. Each night, Ethel Herring led a vespers service. The group met at the top of the fort, Clayton recalled, overlooking the Cape Fear River. "That's when I fell completely under her spell," Clayton recalled. "She was a remarkable, remarkable woman." Clayton remembers Ethel Herring's voice and her stressing the scripture of do justice, love mercy, and walk humbly. "There were a whole lot of us perched up there. It was a very inspiring sort of situation. She was very much a leader." Clayton said those experiences helped lead her to attend college at Wake Forest University, instead of staying at home in South Carolina.

In an interview when her daughter, Ann Herring, became Miss North Carolina in 1960, Ethel Herring talked about her many years working with youth. "My job was to make religion a practical thing to these students—to sustain them through the years away from home. I loved every minute of it."

Ethel Herring's skills were much needed at Watts Street during the war years.

A bulletin board with the names of the "boys in service" was placed in the vestibule of the church: 127 members of the congregation were directly involved in the war effort. J. B. Brame, serving as secretary for the Board of Deacons, relinquished his post when he went to war and then resumed it when he returned. Seven did not come home: Zalph Andrews, Hunter Carpenter, Phillip Adams, William Sally, Demming Ward, and Frank May were killed. Ted Puryear was missing in action. The family of Demming Ward, who died in a plane crash in China, honored him with a plaque under a stained-glass window. The deacons voted for carillon bells in honor of those who served.

In July of 1944, word had come that Zalph Andrews was missing in France. On Sunday evening, October 15, 1944, Herring led a memorial service for Andrews and Carpenter. Andrews had been in training for a career in the ministry before the war came and left behind a young widow and a baby son. He served as an assistant chaplain and was killed in a battle in France while he was working to move wounded soldiers to safety. Carpenter, a marine, had died of wounds received at Guadalcanal.

The loss of all these young men is incalculable. Roughly ten thousand Durham residents served in World War II, and 172 soldiers died, Black and White.

As the fighting and the killing continued, so did church life at Watts Street. Herring asked for more time for his sermons; the deacons debated whether they should have a Loyalty Crusade, a part of the Woman's Christian Temperance Union's program. They left it up to the Evangelicalism Committee. They purchased two lots adjacent to the church with future growth in mind.

Mrs. Lona Sorrel Barbee shines through the minutes as a mainstay of the church and a formidable force. She worked as the church secretary and the educational director, offices that were often combined in the early 20th century. In November 1940, she died of heart trouble at the age of 49. Her husband, D. C. Barbee, was serving as chair of the finance committee and promptly resigned because, the deacon minutes tell us, Mrs. Barbee had been doing all the work.

In early 1941, the women of the church approached the deacons, asking for a larger kitchen and, if possible, to have the toilets moved. The minutes record, "Negative expression in regard to moving toilets. It was suggested that the area of the kitchen might be increased 2 or 3 feet by simply moving the partitions back." The deacons eventually agreed to a remodel and adjourned their meeting to visit the kitchen. In May, the women were asking for a new sink. "Bro. Sally to take proper action to please the ladies in trading for a new sink." By the summer, each of the deacons had chipped in $10 on the remodel. Brother Sally, who seems to have been very involved in the project, announced he would donate $70. They left us no before and after pictures.

"Bro. Brame asked that once and for all, it be settled what the Clerk of the Church is to do," the minutes record. Brother Brame was the clerk of the church. The deacons grumbled that Watts Street was the only Durham church contributing to the Community Fund. They planned to quit. They expressed concern about a trucking terminal at the end of Watts Street and looked for somewhere to buy coal at 60 or 70 cents per ton cheaper.

By the next year, there were more signs the Depression was lifting. In February 1942, they voted to set aside $2,000 and add $50 a week to it. That year, they held the first Vacation Bible School in 12 years, pledging to spend no more than 50 cents a student. They scheduled a revival and looked into bomb insurance for the church. Apparently, more time for Herring's sermons had not met with universal approval and they asked the pastor to have one more hymn in his Sunday services. The custodian was not in good health, and they voted to hire some help for him. They discussed plumbing, termites, and social events. They supported the pastor's efforts with the War Relief Committee and contributed, with other churches, to hiring a bible teacher for the public schools.

In the fall of 1942, the Southern Conference on Race Relations met in Durham. Many prominent Black leaders of the day attended. The conference issued the Durham Manifesto, a document important in Civil Rights history. In it, leaders called for voting rights for Blacks, for fair representation in all branches of government, for a federal anti- lynching law, and an end to segregation. They made the point that Black people were fighting and dying for rights for others they themselves did not have in the United States. Race and racism remained a major issue for the community at large.

Five months after the Manifesto was issued, Ethel Herring led a study for women at Watts Street of a book called The Story of the American Negro. Her co-leader was Eunice Jackson, a Black professor of religious education from Shaw University. Jackson was the first Black woman to graduate from Union Seminary in New York in 1940 and has a chair there endowed in her honor. We have only the reference to the study in a bulletin, but the book itself is remarkable. It was written by Ina Corrine Brown, a White woman. Her book, published in 1936, is a history free of the patronizing tone much history of the time embraced. Her message is not to Black Americans but to White Americans.

"The day is past when Negroes will be grateful for the crumbs which fall from the white man's table," she wrote. Christians have a chance to improve the situation. "This potential leadership of the church will not be realized by evasion, halfway measures, pious wishes, or sentimental generalities. If the church is to lead the way it not only must attack boldly such overt evils as lynching, but it must dig to the roots of the philosophy which underlies discrimination and makes lynchings possible. It must not be content with supporting mission schools and community centers but must face the fact of racial attitudes and practices which deny the Negro full use of public schools, libraries, and other cultural facilities. Both the church as an institution and the individual Christian sooner or later must face the fact that paternalism, enforced segregation, injustice, and discrimination based on race are out of harmony with the basic assumptions of Christian belief. Whether the church of tomorrow shall lead in the field of race relations depends on its willingness to make a courageous choice."

What did the women make of the book and its bold proclamations? Again, they left us no record. On February 20, 1944, Clarence Jordan preached to the church. Jordan was on one of his many fund-raising trips, seeking support for Koinonia Farms, an interracial Christian community he and others founded in 1942 in Americus, Georgia. Turning the pulpit over to him for a Sunday was a radical choice, and one longs for more information. That summer, the women of the church were scheduled to take part in an interracial missionary institute at Mount Vernon Baptist Church, a Black Church. The institute was scheduled for July 9. On July 8, U.S. soldier Booker T. Spicely, a Black soldier stationed at Butner, was shot and killed by a White bus driver. Spicely had objected to moving seats to accommodate White soldiers. The driver was tried for murder and found not guilty.

The world was changing and, as always, Watts Street was changing, too. It was no longer a church defined by its neighborhood. An earlier history records, "The older generation of founding fathers began to relinquish their leadership to a new generation of people who had moved into Trinity Park and refurbished its 50-year-old homes. Dr. Herring saw this change as a good thing and worked to extend the church's membership to the surrounding communities of Hillsboro, Wake Forest, Raleigh, and outlying sections of Durham County."

Herring, always a sensitive man, would sometimes be overcome with emotion while preaching, He would cry during his sermons. This would increasingly be perceived as a problem. Herring would leave in 1946 and take a position at Wake Forest as a professor of religion.

Under his leadership, the church membership had increased from 526 members to 750 members and its budget had more than doubled from $17,000 to $48,000.

To meet the challenges in a postwar world, Watts Street would require a new kind of preacher.

Now these people said they wanted to be liberal, ... Now, what they meant, I found out—I took them more seriously than they intended— they meant they wanted to be able to dance and to drink and play golf, recreate on Sunday without being preached at.

—**Rev. Warren Carr**

The Warren Carr Years, 1946 to 1964

For their fifth pastor, the congregation at Watts Street called a high school football coach with a passion for civil rights and no hesitation in speaking his mind. He would build on the church's openness to social change and set the church on the path of social justice where it remains today.

Warren Carr was from Lexington, Kentucky, and graduated from Transylvania College, where, at 145 pounds, he played football. He went on to Southern Seminary in Louisville, graduating in 1941. His first job was at First Baptist Church in Coeburn, Virginia, where he also coached the high school football team. When the search committee of First Baptist of Princeton, West Virginia, came to hear him preach, he was still sporting a black eye from a brawl with a disgruntled football fan who had insulted Mrs. Carr. The Princeton group, unfazed, called him. He continued to coach high school football and organized an ecumenical youth group open to all races.

When former pastor Rev. Green, back in Durham and working as the editor of the Durham Herald-Sun, heard of Carr's call to Watts Street, he offered advice. Green apparently could not resist boasting a little, telling Carr that Green reached more people in his newspaper columns than Carr would ever reach from the pulpit. Then, more seriously, he wrote about the hard years of the Depression for the church. And then he gave a trenchant account of Watts Street in 1946, the church that Carr would shepherd:

The Carr Family

"Watts Street is not an average church. Only in a few respects is it like other churches I have known. It has a gracious mixture of the poor and the rich. It has its few carping critics, and they don't need to be spotted: They will reveal themselves in time. But to match them it has more fine, sympathetic, understanding and cordial souls than you will find almost anywhere else I know.

"The church needs a lot of loving. It needs an aggressive pastoral relationship extending to all the people. It needs good preaching. The finances of the church will almost take care of themselves. But the church needs to be more missionary-minded. Through the hard years the church has come had it not been for the women, there would have been no missions, or little. The church should render a much greater service to the students at Duke University, but that is not easy. More could be done, though."

43

The Durham that Carr found in 1946 was very different from the town Green had ministered to. From 1920 to 1940, Durham County's population had almost doubled, from 42,000 to 80,000. And that was before the soldiers came during World War II. It would continue to grow by roughly 20 percent over each of the next two decades. Green had increased the membership from 240 when he arrived to 411 when he left. Carr came to a church with 746 members that would grow to 1,346 under his leadership.

But the changes ran much deeper than numbers. The G.I. bill would remake American society. Americans would become more mobile, more educated, and wealthier. Black and White Southerners would abandon the South in massive numbers. The Depression-era families with a small number of children would give way to the Baby Boom. Larger families would flourish and head to church in record numbers. Traditional roles for women and Black people would be challenged in the post-war world.

Carr was happy with his new church, finding a kind of liberal outlook he could work with. "[T]his church had a liberal spirit which former ministers had not caught and built on. They were a people— these people were not content with some of the rigidities of Baptist theology and practice. This is because they were educated." And open to change, Carr said. And although many in the church would disagree with him within the church, when challenges came from those outside, his congregation loyally defended him.

Carr reached out to a new Duke community, growing rapidly and attracting individuals from across the country and around the world in the wake of World War II. Duke students attended the Sunday evening programs at Watts Street and spent many hours at the Carr house, talking theology. "For whatever reason, the ministry to students there was one of trying to make their theology as intellectually respectable as their other disciplines, and in those days, they ate that up," Carr said.

With the influx of new people, both at Duke and in the community, came new ideas. "This whole business of social action began to assert itself," Carr said. As Carr opened Watts Street to interracial meetings and spoke against segregation, he engendered both support and opposition. Many longtime members "were not terribly happy with what took place, [but] they were gritty, great people," Carr said. "And we understood each other completely. I knew that I was going too fast for them; they knew that I would not stay with a segregated church."

Watts Street's archives contain a document, "Duke University Constituents and Watts Street Baptist Church," that gives a rare look into the clash. Founders and longtime Durham residents were proud of their church and its ministry; newcomers, mostly connected with Duke University, had a different vision. They pushed for a more scholarly approach to Christian education, less reliance on Southern Baptist influence, and an end to racial segregation.

The document is undated and unsigned but clearly written by someone on the university side of the battle. We do not know anything about the origins of the report or how it was used. Who was it written for? Was it widely read within the church? An earlier history says the report was written by a spiritual leader in the church and was kept so quiet that neither Carr nor members of the Duke community knew they had been "investigated."

The author identifies the Duke community as students, academics, physicians, and their wives. (It is the 1940s or '50s— apparently, there are no husbands of professionals). He (presumably a he) lists the concerns: a new emphasis on highly trained education personnel offering a "more scholarly approach" to the gospel, displacing longtime members, making them feel "unwanted, unqualified, and ignored.... The established residents of Durham feel that they are progressively losing the power to speak to, influence, or change this trend or to have much effect at all on the ministry of Watts Street Baptist Church." The author turns to numbers to dispute this. Of the 1,056 resident members, only 86 have a Duke tie, or less than 10 percent. Those with Duke ties teach roughly 10 percent of the Sunday School classes but more than 30 percent of the Training School. There is no member of the Duke community on the board of deacons; they are half of the mission committee and one-quarter of the music committee. There is one member of the Duke community who is a member of the WMU.

The author then goes on briefly to discuss the history of the church, built "at undeniable sacrifice and great personal cost ... and maintained through the years of the depression." But this sacrifice does not mean individuals own the church. "We cannot in any measure allow to go unchallenged any idea that we can lay on Jesus Christ or the church demands because of what we have contributed to the upbuilding of this institution. The only charter membership that has meaning in the context of the Kingdom of God is our charter membership in sin."

Longtime members apparently objected to the amount of time Carr was spending with the academic community. The report's author denies that this has caused problems. While "there can be no denial of the popularity and effectiveness with students that Mr. Carr achieved," his ministry to church members has remained far more demanding and church members cannot "show evidence of a less effective ministry to members of this congregation because of his ministry to Duke constituents."

And if church members feel they have been pushed in uncomfortable directions, it is because they should be.

"That the Duke constituency have helped to challenge the church and pushed it in directions not favored by some of the church cannot be denied. But this also must be understood. No Christian church and no Christian can maintain both the integrity of the biblical witness and the church and favor the continuation of racial segregation and its concomitant abuses. This matter is not a mere matter of opinion; it is an irrefutable fact of the Gospel. That we have been so long in recognizing this is only another example of the strength of sin's hold on the life of the church and only reflects the church's shame for its infidelity to the demands of love."

"If the Duke constituency has shown us some inadequacies in ourselves so, also we have demonstrated that education is not the hope for world salvation. That hope is Jesus Christ. Now, once and for all, I say stop this childish bickering. We are capable of much better than this. We have work to do in God's Kingdom."

# # #

Carr kept a high profile in working in God's Kingdom in Durham during his 18 years, particularly his work in civil rights. He served as chair of the Mayor's Committee on Human Relations and as a member of Durham's Interim Committee in Race Relations. In an oral history interview, he claimed the role of mediator, having relationships on both sides of the color line and serving to aid communication. Watts Street's congregation included many influential people, including the mayor and the chair of the city school board and Carr was known to boast of his influence in the city.

Carr also worked with the United Fund, the Child Guidance Council, and the Family Service Board and served as a chaplain-consultant to Alcoholics Anonymous, among others, throughout the years. In Baptist circles, he served on the General Board of State Baptists, was chair of the Baptist Student Committee, and was president of the Yates Baptist Ministers' Association. He also served as a guest instructor at Duke Divinity School, as a trustee for Meredith College, and was a member of the Kiwanis Club. He published several books of sermons, one on baptism, and several articles on the church and race.

He also served as chair of the YMCA board in Durham until they adopted a segregationist bylaw. Carr said his personal policy was that he would not challenge a segregated institution unless they codified the segregation. If they just happened to be all White but had no policy forbidding Black people from joining, he would not challenge it.

I was chairman of the board of the YMCA, and they added the bylaw on segregation to their constitution to keep the blacks out. There were fifteen members of that board; I was chairman, and there nine other members of our church on the board, so ten out of the fifteen were from Watts Street Church," Carr recalled. "The day they did that, I resigned, and one of my members … said, "Warren, this is different from the church." I said, "yeah," but I said, "that initial C, I think, stands for Christian." And I said, "So you'd better take that out of your name."

The national YMCA had abolished segregation in 1946, but it

was not universally adopted. A newspaper article in 1961 on Carr's 15th anniversary in Durham lists his many community roles and memberships and neatly sidesteps the issue of his resignation, saying, "Carr has also been actively interested in the YMCA."

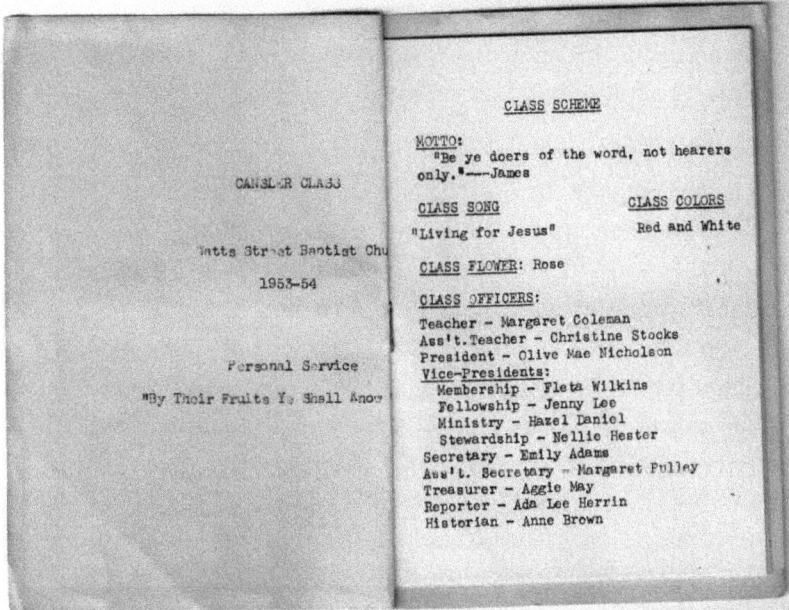

An example of Sunday School classes in the 1950s, with a class motto, a class flower, class colors, and a slate of officers.

Southern Seminary, the alma mater of most of Watts Street's early pastors, was a leader in the civil rights movement from the 1930s through the 1960s. The school was miles ahead of the churches their graduates would lead. A history of Southern says that by the late 1930s, the president and faculty of Southern were anxious to end the institution's segregation practices and began teaching Black students separately. In 1950, the school conducted a survey and found that less than two percent of the students were opposed to racial integration and officially integrated into the seminary the next year. In 1961, Southern Seminary hosted Martin Luther King, Jr.

All Watts Street's pastors to this point had been graduates of Southern, with the lone exception of Green. While Weeks leaves no trace of his feelings, during Herring's tenure, the church had made several steps towards acknowledging the reality of racial discrimination. The only racial reference during Riddick's time came in 1936, when the deacon minutes record, "Treasurer was authorized to pay $5.00 to the Negro Theological Seminary Quartet instead of having them sing in church and take the collection as had been requested."

Apparently, the deacons preferred to pay money rather than allow Black people to lead worship.

Carr marked a radical departure for Watts Street. His Sunday evening meetings with college students included those from Duke and Central. Sometimes, as many as 200 would gather for study, dinner, and a worship service. This was in line with what the North Carolina Baptists were encouraging. "It has been the policy of our BSU convention for the past two years to have present representatives from the leading Negro colleges in the state ... (with) no segregation of the races whatsoever in the auditorium nor in the group seminar," James Ray, the state secretary of the BSU wrote Carr in 1949, asking if Watts Street would host the convention that year. He added that Black students would be housed with Black Baptists in Durham. Watts Street agreed to host. And while the local newspaper covered the BSU convention, it did not mention that it was an interracial meeting, apparently because to mention that was to invite trouble.

Interracial meetings were also happening at some Baptist colleges and seminaries as students struggled to reconcile their faith with Jim Crow laws. Clarence Jordan, one of the founders of Koinonia Farm, a radical experiment for Christians living on a farm outside Americus, Georgia, was touring regularly, speaking at Baptist colleges and seminaries, spreading his anti-racism, anti-poverty message. One Baptist student raised in a racist home remembers struggling with the conflict between her culture and her faith. Hearing Jordan was a clarifying moment for her and sent her into civil rights work. She was far from alone.

These meetings were perceived as a threat by many traditionalists in the Baptist camp. Conservative leaders in North Carolina were concerned that college students were being taught to question rather than to believe. Their fears were confirmed in 1953 when college Baptist leaders invited Nels Feré of Vanderbilt to address the student convention. Feré, considered a liberal, held views to the left of those running the state Baptist convention and state leaders insisted that the invitation be withdrawn. It was.

The next year, the state convention appointed a committee to study liberalism on college campuses and came to focus on three individuals: J. C. Herrin, secretary for the Baptist student organization at UNC-Chapel Hill; James Ray, state student secretary; and Max Wicker, who was the Baptist chaplain for Duke students. Wicker had been ordained at Watts Street two years earlier and worked closely with Carr. The committee met on February 22 and 23 and then summoned the three young men. Resign, they were told, for the good of "the work" or be discharged with a report that would ensure their lack of employability in Baptist circles.

They declined to resign.

There, things hung until Saturday, March 13, when a young Daily Tar Heel reporter named Charles Kuralt broke the story. The banner headline read "Baptists Invite Three Resignations" and included a letter from Dr. M.A. Huggins, executive secretary of the state convention, to several members of Chapel Hill Baptist Church, as University Baptist was then known. The letter asked its recipients to work within their church to get Herrin fired and to destroy the letter as soon as they had read it. The accompanying editorial was entitled "Calvary Hill, 1954" and began, "Three more men of God are about to pay the price of thinking for themselves."

From there, the story, as a later generation would say, went viral. All the state newspapers picked it up, and it was a top story for weeks, eventually making its way into TIME magazine. Samuel Habel, the pastor of Chapel Hill Baptist, clashed openly with Herrin. W. G. Privette, who would go on to resign from the church over this issue, was quoted in the newspaper as saying, "It is well known that the racial issue is the basis for any difference that may exist between Dr. Habel and Herrin."

Carr, who worked closely with Wicker in his work with Duke students, sent an open letter to his congregation, sharing it with the Durham newspapers the morning after the Daily Tar Heel article appeared. He lambasted the state convention, calling for the committee to be dismantled. On Friday, March 19, Carr spoke to hundreds of UNC students in Gerard Hall, decrying the appeasement of the conservatives in the convention. The UNC Baptist group then passed a statement of support for the three ministers.

Within Watts Street, the Board of Education endorsed Carr's position. The deacons were less bold. "After considerable discussion motion was made by C.T. Council and seconded by R. W. Grabarek that no action be taken on the endorsement from the Board of Education. The motion was unanimously carried."

Baptists across the state joined the discussion. Mel Williams, future Watts Street pastor and then a young man in Aberdeen, remembers hearing about the case. The racial issues were downplayed; the young men were not theologically pure, conservatives charged.

The state convention held a long hearing in First Baptist Church of Greensboro on March 30 with hundreds crowding in and, to no one's surprise, fired the three men.

J. C. Herrin, the UNC chaplain, went on to a distinguished career in the Civil Rights movement. His influence was strongly felt in the creation of Olin T. Binkley Baptist church four years later. Max Wicker became a Methodist, serving churches in Virginia. The Chapel Hill church lost about 60 of its members, including several deacons.

The firings took place at the height of the Cold War hysteria. Most newspaper articles about it shared the page with an article about nuclear bombs. The issue of TIME magazine that covered the story had a picture of a nuclear explosion on the cover. The Army-McCarthy hearings were on television that spring.

And on May 17, six weeks after the firings, the long-awaited Brown v. Board of Education ruling was handed down from the Supreme Court, declaring racial segregation in schools to be illegal. The backlash would be ferocious.

###

Warren Carr would boast in later years that Watts Street was the only mainline white church in Durham that was open for Black and White people to meet together after the Brown decision came down. After all, they had hosted interracial meetings at least since 1947, possibly earlier. And at first blush, the Brown ruling enjoyed broad support. The Southern Baptist Convention concluded that Brown was constitutional and supported Christian principles. The state convention in Charlotte that year encouraged congregations to push on with integration and to face the issue of race and the equality of all before God. They expressed confidence that local congregations would do what is right. Watts Street held a church-wide discussion of the Brown decision at a church night meeting in November of 1955, but they left us no details of what was said.

With the announcement of the Brown decision and a sustained history of welcoming Black visitors to the church, Carr decided it was time to ask the deacons to create a policy to handle the situation that might arise should a Black person present themselves for membership. After some initial opposition to having a policy, by September, the deacons had produced a policy:

"Should the occasion arise wherein a negro should present himself for membership at one of the Sunday worship services without previous communication of this desire to the Church, the pastor shall invite a motion from the members that the matter be referred to the Board of Deacons for consideration."

The deacons unanimously adopted this policy, which Carr supported, and announced it to the church. In the 1950s, church policy was still decided by the deacons and the pastor and then announced to the rest of the church. There were vehement objections from members who called it a Jim Crow membership. The church would continue to debate the policy for the next 14 years, but the policy stood.

While Watts Street apparently had many Black visitors over these years and welcomed those who came as part of Civil Rights initiatives, no Black Christians presented themselves for membership, despite personal invitations from Carr.

At a church meeting in November 1962, one member, the Rev. Charles Wellborn, "made the motion that all persons regardless of race who present themselves for membership" be accepted. The church membership voted to table the motion.

Carr, who had missed that meeting, wrote to Vivian A. Parks, chair of deacons, upset that the congregation apparently tried to avoid the issue. If so, he wrote, "I will find this to be an impossible situation in which to minister." But he did not support Wellborn's motion, instead defending the policy already in place. "It deals honestly, openly, and realistically with a difficult situation. To treat a matter that is unusual, embracing the conditioned emotions and attitudes of southern people, both Negro and White, as if it were not unusual is unrealistic and unwise."

It was not the most Christian of policies, he admitted, but "it is better to accept this judgment upon ourselves and move toward the higher ethical level with a sense of compromise at a slower pace than some may desire but which conserves your progress and does not retreat from our present position." Another proposal aimed at fairness had been to require all prospective members to come before the deacons in the manner currently required of non-existent Black members. Carr insisted that policy "can be nothing but a façade and the spirit behind it could cause undesirable results. Whatever is done should be done openly with the realization that the judgment of God, as it comes, need not find us hiding out but in the light of open confrontation."

In a church meeting the next year, a motion was made to allow the whole church to vote on any proposed membership by a Black person. The motion was voted down.

The two-track membership policy, never used, was abolished in 1968, in the wake of Martin Luther King Jr.'s assassination. With one dissenting vote.

# # #

With the legal barriers to segregation removed, the question of implementation loomed. On May 6, 1955, Watts Street hosted an interracial public forum on "integration in education, especially as pertains to our local school situation." There was a panel of three: Professor Hornell Hart, a Duke sociologist. Professor Rose Butler Browne, an education professor at NCCU, and James C. N. Paul of the Institute of Government at Chapel Hill. The forum, which included discussion and questions from the audience, was sponsored by the Intercollegiate Fellowship for Religion in Life, an interdenominational group of Duke, North Carolina College, and UNC students.

No details of the forum remain for us. And apparently, it was not the only interracial meeting held at the church that month. The deacon minutes recorded: "The interracial meeting held at the church on Sunday, May 15, was discussed, but no action was considered necessary."

By the next year, those opposed to integration had made plans. North Carolina, like many southern states, looked for a legal way around school integration. State leaders had created the Pearsall Plan, which offered parents new tools to avoid sending their children to integrated schools. Student assignments were left up to local school boards.

The state was set to vote on the Pearsall plan on September 8, 1956. Carr, opposed to the plan, asked the deacons for permission to hold a churchwide meeting on the referendum. On August 20, the deacons met for a lengthy discussion without Carr present and decided to go on record against Carr having a meeting "as it would offend many people." Perhaps fearing their fate if they sent a single deacon to tell Carr, they appointed a committee of three for the task.

The Pearsall plan was approved by North Carolina voters by a margin of 4 to 1 and effectively delayed significant integration for more than a decade.

Not that people quit trying. The newspaper carried a photo of the Rev. Douglas E. Moore, pastor of Asbury Temple Methodist Church, praying with some students before they tried to be served in the white section at the Royal Ice Cream Parlor at Roxboro and Dowd on June 23, 1957. They entered the business, declined to leave the front of the store reserved for white customers, and they were arrested. Other attempts were made at entering a public library deemed for whites only, playing tennis or swimming at whites-only city parks, and seeking to sit on the floor at the popular Carolina Theater instead of on the balcony.

And there were some small victories. Three Black students enrolled at UNC in 1955, all of them from Durham. Lawsuits against the local school board led to some token integration. Church member Eloise Williamson, who grew up at Watts Street, remembers starting the school year at Brogden Jr High in 1959 and seeing police cars with flashing lights in the distance, headed for the school. They were there to escort two Black students into all-white Brogdon. Years later, Williamson and one of those students taught together at another school.

In July 1958, a disgruntled suitor of one of Carr's four daughters hurled a smoke bomb into the Carr home. In declining to bring any charges, the district attorney downplayed the seriousness of the incident, saying it was neither a bomb nor a grenade. Carr said he had no previous relationship with the boys involved except trying to help them. He also said there would be some "red faces" in Durham because as word spread of the incident, people assumed it was because of his work on the Mayor's Committee on Human Relations.

Another incident that resulted from his work on racial issues involved vandalism to the church. Carr would tell the story repeatedly and proudly over the years. He recalled that Marion Wiggins, the church custodian, came to him early one Friday morning and said someone had painted "Go to hell, you n [sic] lover" on the front doors to the church. Carr instructed the custodian to paint over it. But the next morning, there was a similar, more personal message: "Go to hell, you n——-lovin' Warren Carr." Again, Carr instructed that it be painted over. And again, it reappeared the next morning—a Sunday morning. This time, it said, "Go to hell, you n——-lovin' church."

Carr decided it was a compliment and left it at least for a while. He admitted not everyone in the church viewed it as a compliment.

Morning Herald

Rebel Weariness

Correspondent W. L. Ryan sees signs of rebel weariness and government realization of futility in continued Lebanese battling. For details, see story on 7-A.

DURHAM, N.C., TUESDAY, JULY 8, 1958 — 18 PAGES—2 SECTIONS — PRICE DAILY 5¢; SUNDAY 15¢

Baptist Parsonage Is Target Of Smoke Bomb; None Hurt

Police Probing Blast At Warren Carr Home

By GEORGE LOUGEE
Herald Staff Writer

A firecracker-like smoke bomb was hurled early Monday morning against the home of the Rev. Warren Carr, pastor of Watts Street Baptist Church.

No one was injured in the 12:30 a. m. blast at the Carr home, 1024 Urban Ave., which serves as the parsonage for his church.

The Rev. Mr. Carr is chairman of the Mayor's Committee on Human Relations, a group created to promote harmony between the races here.

Det. Capt. W. E. Gates said the explosive, about one inch in diameter, apparently bounced off a window screen and discharged, causing a sharp report and giving off a yellowish smoke which was pulled into the broken window by an exhaust fan operating inside the home.

Minister Heading Human Relations Group Unruffled

The headline in 1958 when the Reverend Warren Carr's home was hit with a smoke bomb during his time on the Mayor's Committee on Human Relations.

Some in the church may have shared some of the vandal's sentiments despite Carr's best efforts. While Carr preached an open and inclusive gospel every Sunday, he said he never preached a sermon on integration. Instead, he hoped, "If I had anything to do with it, it was to declare the faith which made segregation ridiculous." Years later, he still marveled at some of the responses his congregation shared. "They would say to me, 'Well, we know we're still segregationists, but we know that we can't defend it on Bible or faith.' I mean, they would say that."

In 1959, members of Watts Street's Women's Missionary Union approached the deacon board to share their opinions on integration. The members of Circle 11 wrote that segregation was incompatible with what the church stood for. "The cultural and social problems that would arise from racial integration in our church loom ominously before many. We suggest, however, that these problems, no matter how difficult, must be faced with the courage of our convictions and freely discussed among the members of our church with all the Christian grace and intelligence at our command."

The deacons responded politely with their thanks and a copy of the September 20, 1954, meeting where they had set the policy on admitting Black people to church. In 1962, the WMU held a service on March 9, a national interracial day of prayer.

Many people say that during this period, it was not unusual to see Black people attending church services at Watts Street, but hard data is difficult to come by. In the late 1950s, five Black people came to worship at Watts Street. The 75th history tells us that John Stone was ushering that morning, and he steered the group towards the balcony. When they objected, no doubt thinking about the many establishments that had relegated their race to the balcony, Stone informed them that the seats below were full and they had come too late to get a seat there. If they came back the next week at an earlier time, he said he would happily seat them down in front. They did come back, he did seat them down front, and Watts Street enhanced its reputation as an "open church."

As the sit-in movement swept the country in 1961, there were kneel-ins in churches, starting on Palm Sunday and going through May. Several churches in Durham sent their deacons out to block Black people from entering. According to an oral history with Temple Baptist Church's pastor, no one went to Watts Street because it was known to be open, and the point was to test the welcome in uncertain places.

Watts Street's deacons continued to approve interracial meetings at the church and to study the issue throughout the 50s and 60s. In July 1963, the deacons received a letter from the state Baptist Student Union saying that a Black Baptist would be enrolling at Duke: will that make a difference for the BSU that meets at Watts Street? The deacons replied that nothing would change, and they would continue to work with BSU as before.

A mysterious exception to the policy of welcome occurred in 1964, when Julius H. Corpening, pastor of Temple Baptist Church and friend of Warren Carr, wrote Watts Street asking if the Durham's Minister's Association could use Watts Street's sanctuary the third

Sunday in February to hold an interracial service as part of their observance of Brotherhood Sunday. The deacons denied the request, saying they did not know enough about the group, raising questions as to how the deacons could not know enough about their own local ministerial association. Sunday School classes and individuals wrote letters to the deacons, calling their action unchristian. At the next church meeting, member Charles Wellborn asked for an explanation of the deacons' actions, leading to a discussion but no action.

#

Carr was very aware and appreciative of the platform his church gave him and the freedom he felt in the pulpit to preach the gospel as he saw it. A free pulpit was something no church could guarantee, he said. A preacher had to earn it every time he stepped into his pulpit to preach.

And while Carr was one of several Durham ministers speaking up for civil rights, many ministers wanted to do more but feared backlash from conservative congregations.

Duke Divinity School professor Waldo Beach addressed the ministerial association in Durham "and stood there for an hour to tell us what cowards we were. Why we were not ... the kind of prophets we ought to be," Carr recalled. When Beach finished and asked for questions, Carr recalled he stood up and said he had no questions, but he did have a comment. "I think we just heard a prophet with tenure. When you don't have tenure, it's a little different."

The Watts Street congregation got pressure from others in Durham about Carr's actions. "What they would say is, You're letting the bars down" against segregation, Carr said. "But they told those people to mind their own business time and again. Downtown and businesses, civic clubs, they would even say, Why don't you get rid of your preacher?" implying that racial turmoil would go away if Carr went away. Watts Street members would respond, "We'll deal with our preacher. You ... paddle your own canoe. And they were steadfast.... This wasn't the Duke people; those were the bankers and lawyers and doctors and business people."

Watts Street was "just a church which I think God raised up for the day," Carr recalled. "And so they were—they were tough."

As proud as he was of the support of the church, Carr later noted that he had been prepared to resign whenever he took a controversial stand. "We tried to be civil with each other when we knocked heads in the city. Chairman of the school board, for example, was a member of my church was a confirmed segregationist so far as public education was concerned. When I became chairman of the mayor's committee on human relations [sic], we knocked heads all the time. That never destroyed our relationship as friends and never destroyed our fellowship as brothers in Christ in the church."

Carr recounted the story of a rich man in his congregation who was often ready to fire Carr for his liberal stands. "Every time I'm about to do that, my daughter-in-law tells me that you [Carr] went out at two o'clock in the morning and picked my son out of a ditch, dead drunk, and took him to your house and put him to bed. How can I fire you?" the man grumbled.

And Carr had advice for young pastors who wanted to speak out about injustice:

The greatest advice that I felt I could give to any liberal pastor who wanted to make some influence there was, Buddy, you be sure they can't get you for something else. If you get fired, you make them fire you for this position. You see, I've always been impatient with liberals who don't do their homework and who are incompetent and who think because they got some great liberal idea on one aspect of the gospel or humanism or whatever that, they've got a license to be sloppy—to be sloppy in their preaching, to be sloppy in their pastoral work.

# # #

As Durham changed in the postwar years, so did things within the church. In 1948, Watts Street created a board of education for the church, with four programs: Sunday School, Sunday Night Training School, Music, and Missions. One of its first actions was to issue a report critical of the church's music. It was too expensive, too provincial, and out of touch with the church's needs, the report charged. In one month, the organist, the minister of music, and the minister's assistant—three-quarters of the staff—all resigned. The church used the sudden vacancies to remake their music and educational programs.

Previously, the church had assigned responsibilities for the education programs to a woman (it was always a woman) hired as the minister's assistant. She also worked as an office administrator. In 1949, following the mass resignation, the church hired Miss Mary Islan Crumpler to be a minister of education at $250 a month. (She is the first to be listed as a minister, not a director, but most staff who did that job were listed as a director until 1964, when John Davis was listed as a Minister of Education, as is everyone to hold the post after him.) Crumpler set to work with a will, making changes. In the new programs, boys and girls no longer met in separate classrooms; children were grouped by their grade in school and not their age; a young adult department was added; and the problem of finding qualified teachers increased. Parents were required to attend conferences with their child's Sunday School teachers monthly. Carr was pleased with the improvement in Christian education at the church. He pointed out that children's test scores were up, and he gave much of the credit to the Sunday School superintendent, W. E. Stanley.

A youth retreat at Camp Kanata, led by Youth Director Jean Dula.

Curriculum became an issue. Watts Street's Training School—for some reason, they called it school rather than union—relied on the Southern Baptist materials for elementary-school children and young adults; for other ages, Carr wrote supplemental materials. Some Sunday School classes used the SBC curriculum. But, dissatisfaction with the Southern Baptist curriculum was growing, and several committees were appointed to study the matter. In 1964, the church began to use the United Church of Christ materials.

Revivals were a standard part of church life in Carr's years of ministry, but he was never a fan. Deacon minutes from February 1950 include criticism from other Baptist churches that Watts Street has not been holding revivals in recent years.

The basis of this criticism was that we were not cooperating with the other Baptist churches in the city. The pastor expressed his willingness to conduct a revival meeting if members of the church so desired but frankly stated he considers our present method (of continuous revival services and an invitation to membership at the end of each service) superior to a week of special services.... There were expressions of confidence in our present method, and it was the consensus of our Board that we should continue it.

The next year, the Southern Baptist Convention called for simultaneous revivals in the spring. In January, Carr said he was having difficulty in finding a pastor for a revival and, again, questioned the worth of revivals. In February, he still had not found a revivalist for Watts Street. In March, the situation had not changed, and the deacons said Carr should conduct whatever services he wanted however he saw fit. In April, Carr reported that a revival had been held. The deacons voted him their thanks. Carr apparently agreed to hold one more revival during his tenure, November 6-11, 1960.

#

The 1950s and early '60s were a boom time for church attendance more generally, and Watts Street was no exception. Folding chairs were added to the center aisle, and an overflow room was created just off the sanctuary. Watts Street bought a speaker system and began holding a second service on Sunday morning. "The pastor is not at all enthusiastic over the prospect," the minutes from the meeting where the decision was made to add a service. Carr was taking the minutes at that meeting.

The church grew physically as well as in numbers. Over the years, the church had purchased several houses and lots that adjoined the church property. When Carr arrived in 1946, he began encouraging the deacons to put an educational wing on the church. It was completed and opened in 1954. This capital project also brought air- conditioning throughout the church complex, bringing an end to the era of hand-held church fans with their memorable advertising. Marion Ham, a church member and architect who had drawn up the plans for an educational wing, had also made plans to enlarge the sanctuary. Despite the fact that the sanctuary was very crowded most Sundays, deacons found "a great deal of sentiment attached to our present sanctuary, which we respect." The enlargement plan was dropped.

The role of women would shift during Carr's time at Watts Street in important ways. On October 9, 1951, the deacons considered a request from the WMU to make women eligible for service as deacons. With no opposition, the deacons voted to amend the bylaws to allow women to serve as deacons and created a slate of women candidates for four new positions, with one woman listed as an alternate. (The deacon board was growing steadily to keep pace with the increase in church members at the time and was due for four new positions.)

Less than ten days later, they called a special meeting and rescinded the decision to allow women to be deacons. They alleged that no women were willing to serve. It is difficult to believe that the WMU would have asked for women to serve without having individuals in mind; the reversal must have stung.

The fall church meeting minutes that year say that a man read a letter from the WMU without recording what the letter was about or why a man was reading a letter from an exclusively women's organization. A change in how the WMU would give money to the church was referred to but not explained. There was a mention of "not entirely a unified budget church." Money raised by women and their desire to control where it went was often a source of conflict in Protestant churches. In 1961, there was a proposal to change the WMU bylaws and incorporate it into Watts Street. It is not clear why. The next year for the first time, the deacons approved the leaders of the WMU.

In 1956, on the occasion of his tenth anniversary at Watts Street, Carr took a moment to look back in satisfaction. The education program had improved, and the worship service was more meaningful, with its music and symbols, he said, "even though [the members] like flowers on the communion table." That was apparently something Carr did not like. And more importantly, "I believe that we have passed the stage of being afraid to scrutinize the Christian faith in its traditional categories. We are no longer encumbered with a stifling literalism in our approach to scriptures."

On August 20, 1956, Carr was interviewed for an article in Life magazine about pastor burnout. He said that he gave his parishioners a survey asking how much time they thought their pastor should devote to each of his duties. It came to a total of 82 hours a week.

Carr, like several of the pastors before him, was not successful in establishing a quiet time in the sanctuary before the service began. Earlier bulletins and newsletters request reverence and calm as the congregation gathers, with deacons instructed to encourage compliance. For many years, Carr made sure the bulletin included a reminder until 1954, when he got a call from a member.

The next bulletin carried this message: "Perhaps you have noticed the inscription at the top of our bulletin, which comes from Emerson. It has read, "I like the silent church before the service begins." We had copied this from the bulletin of another church and did not check it thoroughly. Not long ago, one of our members called me rather late at night. He, believe it or not, had been reading Emerson. He explained that he could not wait to inform me that the bulletin selection had been lifted out of the context of one of Emerson's sentences. I was then informed that the entire sentence read, "I like the silent church before the service begins better than any preaching," Carr wrote.

"I am now looking for another inscription to be placed at the beginning of our bulletin."

In June of 1955, the worship committee recommended no changes to the baptistry "and that the pastor not wear a robe." The deacons often discussed overflow crowds. In 1957, a revised covenant was adopted. In 1958, the Sunday School committee was upset with the lack of preparation and interest from junior and high school classes. They decided to go back to testing to force students to study.

While happy with the progress made in the education program, the church apparently had trouble keeping an employee to oversee the programs. In September 1948, Carr asked if the deacons would please consider hiring a man on their next try, apparently believing gender was the problem. They did hire a man in the next few years, and the situation did not improve.

In a 1962 letter, the chair of the deacons laid out the problems in keeping an education director bluntly, perhaps to someone who was considering taking the position.

The first left after a definite clash with the pastor, which after brewing for some time came to a climax in her dismissal.... The second left to marry. The third left for work in which she would have more opportunities to meet men, matrimony in mind. All three of these are women. The fourth, a man, felt that in certain efforts to introduce changes, he did not have the support of the pastor after having been led to expect such support in his opinion. The pastor, I may add, admits that in one instance, this was true but denies it in another. It should also be pointed out that this person came with a self-imposed limitation on areas of service, saying on one occasion that there were only three churches in the Southern Convention in which he could work, Watts Street being one of them. I am afraid his disillusionment on this point came early.

The deacon minutes from Carr's tenure continued standard themes from the church's life: It is hard to find enough members willing to do the work of the church, they need a better system of delivering communion, and the NC Baptist convention expects a large contribution to the "Wake Forest Enlargement Campaign." (An earlier committee appointed to raise money for Wake Forest College had to be reconfigured when church members objected vehemently that the committee consisted only of Wake Forest alums.) In 1961, Carr asked for a study of the relationship with the Girl Scout troop, noting, "There seems to be a lack of adequate supervision." Ushers reported problems with getting people to settle down quietly before the services. A class in personal witnessing was offered; an invitation was issued to a Jewish rabbi to speak at an evening service, and adult education "remains a crying need." The next year, the deacons studied possible affiliation with the American Baptist Convention and looked for a Cuban refugee to help. It took several tries, but eventually, the church found a person from Cuba to help settle into a new life in North Carolina. Carr reported that a church in Jacksonville, Florida, had called him and that he declined.

As the church continued its missions and meetings, the 1950s were giving way to the 1960s in ways that would dramatically affect the church and the larger society. For the church meeting in July 1960, Carr wrote: "It is growingly evident that the 'religious boom' has started to subside. This means that churches in general will face greater difficulty in enlisting support for their ministry than has been the case over the past decade It is already apparent that the effects are being felt throughout the life of our church." He placed part of the blame on himself for "having become too involved in the community and denomination," proposing to "give up a number of such responsibilities whenever possible so that I can give more time to study." He also pledged to overcome "my congenital aversion to administrative detail."

The church launched a large study of its own strengths and weaknesses and laid out plans. The report covered a wide range of issues. All members were invited to participate in one of six groups. Among the issues discussed were relations with the Southern Baptists, the adoption of the revised covenant and a proposal to read it once a month in church, and the need for "quiet reverence" in the sanctuary before the service began each Sunday. Families were encouraged to sit together during the service and to come to at least one service on Sunday or be considered in violation of the covenant. (There is no hint as to what happens to those found in violation of the covenant.) The Education Committee stressed to parents that educating children was really the parent's job. Deacons were required to visit those who were capable of teaching but declined to do so. They were also to clarify the nature of the responsibilities of positions before members accepted them and to confront members who might attempt to quit. The church needed more opportunities for adults, more concern for worldwide and local missions, and more money and training in witnessing. Members were encouraged to have personal and family devotions.

It was a wide-ranging report.

# # #

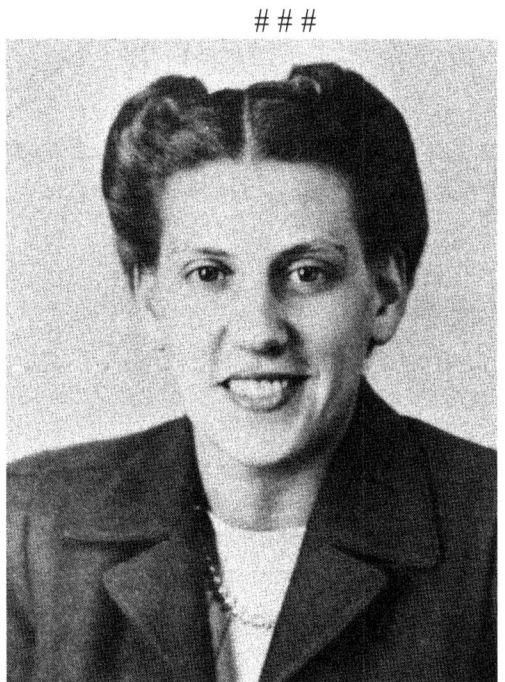

The Reverend Addie Davis, the first woman ordained in the Southern Baptist Convention.

That same year, a young woman named Addie Davis joined Watts Street. Her path to Watts Street had been a long one. She had grown up in a Baptist Church in Covington, Virginia, attended Meredith College in Raleigh, and then worked as the Education Director at a Baptist Church in Elkin and then as Dean of Women at Alderson- Broadus College. She felt a call to ministry and applied to and was accepted at Duke and Yale Divinity schools, but her father's death meant she returned to Covington for a decade and helped her mother run the family's furniture store. During that time, she served as an interim at Lone Star Baptist Church for six months. When her mother retired, she was ready to pursue her calling again.

She enrolled at Southeastern Baptist Theological Seminary and looked for a church that would consider the radical step of ordaining a woman. She found Watts Street and Warren Carr.

"I felt that I had a friend in Warren Carr He said it sort of threw him at first, but being the kind of man he is, he said yes. And he laid the groundwork very patiently and quietly in the church among the people, and I am sure in the association among fellow pastors," Davis recalled.

Carr said he told her he could make no promises, but he added she should let the church get to know her and suggested that they would be open to the possibility. She joined, and at the February 1963 deacons' meeting, they approved a license to preach for her, a precursor to ordination. Then, she had to wait out a snowstorm that postponed the meeting to wait and see if the church would approve her. "That was a rough two weeks for me, waiting to see if I would be approved. And the church approved. It was a large business meeting, and they had been notified If anyone was opposed, then they must not have voted because I think the vote was unanimous as far as we can tell. There were well over one hundred people in attendance," she said. She preached at the evening church service on May 5.

The next hurdle was ordination. In her note of thanks to Vivian Parks, chair of the deacons, Davis pressed the issue. "We spoke briefly of future plans for ordination, and of course, I am willing to wait for the will of the Church in this matter," she said. "From my own viewpoint I have wondered if it would be feasible to consider any plans for ordination in the immediate future.... I had hoped for ordination by or on June 30th so that some particular professors and friends could attend."

But Watts Street did not rush to ordain her. Having a call—or job offer—from a church was not necessarily a precursor to ordination, but Watts Street's deacons wanted Davis to have such a call before they ordained her. She pushed back.

"I have also recognized the fact that some of our men are

ordained before they have a call to a church," she wrote. "I do not expect the getting started to be easy, and this is another reason I have wondered if ordination would be beneficial in this regard."

Parks disagreed. "It is the feeling of the Deacons and the Pastor that ordination should await a definite call to a church. In our view, the service or ordination would, at that time be more meaningful and more in keeping with its purpose. We do not believe that the absence of ordination would be a negative factor in your being called by a church."

There, things stayed for months until a call came from a church in Vermont. Still, Davis would face obstacles. But Carr and the deacons agreed it was time. Ordination would involve an examination by a group of Baptist pastors, and Carr made a point of selecting carefully, asking that those who served on the board be open to the possibility of ordaining a woman. Carr would tell the story many times in the years to come.

And they assured me that they would not be prejudiced. We had a young man that we examined first that day. He stood a lousy examination theologically. Then Addie came, and she was superb, and of course, when they asked her about the virgin birth and those kinds of arguments, you know, she came through with flying colors. And then, as you might expect, the old prejudices of the brethren began to rise, and when we were discussing voting approval of her, two gentlemen said they couldn't do it, that she was a woman, and that they could not break precedent, so forth and so on. And I think the thing that turned the whole thing around was a young Duke student ... part-time associate in the divinity school, and he said, "Brethren, I've never been on this kind of thing before," but he said—he'd been examined, he was an ordained minister—but he said, "I'm a little confused. You gentlemen have been so concerned that our candidates believe without question that a virgin bore the Word. Now," he says, "you're hung up on a virgin preaching the Word."

Carr said the statement broke the tension, leading to laughter and Davis's approval.

Davis didn't leave us her account of the examination or her

impression of her examiners. She was one of the first six women to earn a Bachelor of Divinity degree and had written an academic paper making the case for women preachers. She was keenly aware she was the first. For Southern Baptists, this decision was a historic moment, although one they would later try to disavow.

Addie Davis was ordained at Watts Street in August 1964, and members of her future church in Vermont came down for the service. She was 47 when she embarked on what would be a distinguished 41- year career in ministry.

Davis's ordination service represents a high point in the history of Watts Street Baptist Church. Davis wrote Parks soon afterward: "It would be impossible for me to find words adequate to express my appreciation for what the Watts Street Baptist Church has meant to me in every respect, and how especially grateful I am for the wholehearted support they have given to me in this endeavor to enter the ministry."

"The ordination service was meaningful to many of us present as it was to you," Parks responded. "I am glad to have been able to be a participant in this service, which opened the door for what I am confident will be a fruitful ministry. Please be assured of our continuing interest and support during the days ahead."

The church had come a long way and would celebrate the anniversary of this milestone in the years to come. A news article on the 30th anniversary of her ordination quotes Carr: "We did not ordain Addie to be the first. We did not ordain her because she was a woman. We ordained her because she convinced me that the Lord would not let her rest until she was a preacher."

The path to having women deacons in the church would be a little longer. A deacons' report in March 1962 calls for the deacon board to be increased in members, with at least four women serving. There is no hint as to what happened to that report, and no women were added to the deacon board. Carr said multiple attempts were made, and as in 1951, no women were willing to serve.

It would be 1965, the year after Addie Davis was ordained, that Watts Street would finally get its first woman deacon, Delories

Atkins, and for several years she would serve as the only woman on the board.

As almost his last service to Watts Street, Carr attended the Southern Baptist Convention in Atlantic City, New Jersey, in May 1964. Baptists of all stripes were gathering to celebrate a jubilee, the 150 years of Baptists in the United States. The SBC and the ABC were meeting simultaneously and the possibility of mending the 1845 split over slavery was being considered. Freedom Summer in Mississippi was about to get underway, and Dr. Martin Luther King Jr. was speaking at the ABC. The Rev. Billy Graham attended. The Civil Rights Act was before Congress and Vice President Hubert Humphrey issued a statement to the Baptists, asking for them to push for Civil Rights. President Johnson had said the Southern Baptists held the key to making civil rights a reality. The Christian Life Commission of the SBC brought a recommendation that the SBC endorse civil rights.

They declined. And they declined to fellowship with other Baptist groups.

Carr reported back to his church at a July meeting that, "I must say, regrettably, that this was the worst convention I have ever attended."

Six weeks later, Johnson signed the Civil Rights Act of 1964 into law hours after Congress had passed it.

Later that year, Carr accepted a call to be the pastor of Wake Forest Baptist Church in Winston-Salem, leaving behind a different church than the one he found in 1946.

Warren Carr shaped Watts Street in many ways. He was a leader in race relations, but he was far from a one-issue preacher. He insisted that morality was much broader than race. He believed in the transforming power of the gospel in all aspects of life. He was not known for his modesty. It was said that if the convention was on fire and Carr made a motion that the messengers evacuate, he would not be able to get a second. He had his fans and his detractors and his faith.

His influence is felt still.

Some of us could work at trying to understand that freedom is not to be equated with complete disregard of the Christian tradition. Many of us could try to come to terms with the truth that repetition of the past shouldn't be equated with faithfulness to it.

Rev. Robert McClernon

The Robert McClernon Years, 1965 to 1987

For their next pastor, Watts Street called the Rev. Robert McClernon, who had been serving as minister of education at Myers Park Baptist Church in Charlotte. Carlyle Marney, a pastor well-known for his outspoken and liberal ways, was the senior pastor at Myers Park.

McClernon was originally from Springfield, Missouri, and was a graduate of Drury College. He was not a product of Southern Seminary in Louisville, like so many of his predecessors at Watts Street. His divinity degree was from the University of Chicago, in cooperation with the Chicago Theological Seminary, an institute that prides itself on a history of "progressive firsts and historic social justice." He came to Durham in July 1965 with his wife JoNell and their three children, ready for the challenge.

He arrived in the midst of the turbulent 1960s. The Civil Rights Act had been signed into law the summer before he came, stripping away legal fictions protecting segregation. The year after his arrival, the U.S. Supreme Court declared the Pearsall Plan, the law that had delayed desegregation in North Carolina, unconstitutional, clearing the way for meaningful integration. The Tonkin Gulf Resolution had been passed by Congress in August 1964, and the massive buildup of U.S. troops in Vietnam began. The postwar boom in church attendance was declining due to the anti- establishment feeling of the time. TIME magazine ran a famous cover in April 1966, asking, "Is

God Dead?" Pundits debated, and church leaders called for renewal and rededication.

The McClernon family at Watts Street when they arrived in 1965.

It was a troubled time, and McClernon faced it squarely. A later tribute from the church to McClernon said, "Bob brought with him a questioning, searching, and loving attitude based upon a sound and solid confidence and belief in the God we all seek   Consistently,

Sunday after Sunday, he has brought us sermons that do not allow us to escape."

His direct approach was not always appreciated, however. In July 1971, McClernon wrote the congregation of his first six years at Watts Street: "I wouldn't want to live them over again, and neither, I imagine, would you. They were difficult for almost all of us. Some of the pain we experienced was unnecessary and avoidable. Much of it was probably inevitable, for these six years were not hospitable ones in which to try to keep on becoming a church of Christ. Change and conflict confronted us in the world on every hand."

# # #

Shortly after his arrival, McClernon told the deacons that the church was not where it should be in many areas. The congregation needed a new seriousness about its spiritual life, its missions, and its fellowship. As always, the budget was an issue, and McClernon expressed concern about the "present financial situation as symptomatic of something wrong with the congregation." He said two factors appeared to be responsible; first, the diffuseness of commitment on the part of the congregation, and second, the lack of anything adventuresome about the budget. As a relative newcomer, he said that he "sensed no wholeness in the congregation, a lack of spirit of community," the March 1966 deacon notes record. He proposed more fellowship, retreats, and study. "More people are expressing a concern that Watts Street be a unified church. It is important that we soon be found doing some things that we are not now doing."

The next month, the deacons asked everyone to increase their pledges by 20 percent. Deacon Homa Freeman listed several reasons why he thought the church might be struggling financially: disagreement with the "liberal stance" of the church, a wait-and-see attitude about the new pastor, concern over the new curriculum, or "too little challenge being offered." Freeman said that Watts Street might be a "second generation" church, more dependent on a second generation with less earning power than its founding generation. The church has not been "educated" to keep up with the church's growth and inflation, he said.

The new curriculum was a challenge McClernon faced almost immediately. Shortly before his arrival, the church had agreed to use the United Church of Christ curriculum. Some were not pleased with this choice. At his first church meeting in August 1965, McClernon wrote of his support of the decision. The church had been using a hodge-podge of different curriculums, and choosing one was an attempt to have a unified education program. The most important part not covered in the UCC materials, from a Baptist point of view, was Believer's Baptism. But the local church could supplement the curriculum, and the SBC offerings so many used were no longer an option for Watts Street.

"There are a number of factors that we need to face in Southern Baptist life," McClernon wrote. "In 1963, the SBC was composed of 32,126 churches. Of that number, only 9,845 were in cities of a population of 2,500 or greater." Most were in rural communities of people with less education. "The Southern Baptist Convention produced its literature and programs for the majority and aims at the lowest common denominator. This is perhaps as it ought to be. But we would be very unwise to think that material that would be timely, relevant, and adequate for this rural constituency would also meet the needs satisfactorily of this congregation." He stressed that Watts Street was, and intended to remain, a Baptist church, but "a good Baptist church is not necessarily one that follows the Convention programs developed by Nashville."

# # #

Like Carr before him, McClernon believed segregation and racial discrimination were antithetical to the gospel message. At the 1965 SBC convention, the group had apparently overcome its reservations from the year before and called on all its member churches to live out their faith by working to end all forms of racial discrimination. They suggested churches honor a brotherhood Sunday and reach out to Black Christians.

For his first brotherhood Sunday at his new church, McClernon was part of the first known racial pulpit exchange in Durham with the Rev. Lorenzo Lynch of White Rock Baptist Church. White Rock has a long and proud history in the civil rights struggle and Durham politics. The Rev. Martin Luther King Jr. preached there on February 16, 1960, during the sit-ins.

"What is probably a new departure from the established custom which prevails between the white and Negro churches of Durham will move off in a new direction here Sunday, February 20," wrote the Carolina Times, a Black weekly newspaper in Durham of the exchange. "Both ministers are considered among the best prepared of the city, and a large and enthusiastic congregation is expected to be on hand at each service."

The Durham Herald Sun ran a short article headlined: White, Negro Pastor To Exchange Pulpits.

Lynch preached to the Watts Street congregation "On Some Challenges of Negro Local Churches in the Twentieth Century." The program for the service included copies of the SBC's statements, The Racial Crisis and On Human Relations, both calls for action to end racism in all forms. At the same time, McClernon preached to the White Rock congregation a sermon entitled "No Longer a Stranger."

McClernon was pleased with the events. "Our recent celebration of Brotherhood Sunday increased immeasurably my confidence in the congregation's ability to rise, even if only momentarily, above the entanglements of 350 years of cultural betrayal of Jesus Christ in the matter of brotherhood. I do not intend to make more of this than ought to be made of it, yet it seems to me that the response of our people was for the most part Christian and if not Christian, at least stoically courteous," McClernon wrote to the congregation.

McClernon was an invited guest at Lynch's installation ceremony in April; the featured speaker was Carlyle Marney, McClernon's former colleague. But there were no more pulpit exchanges between McClernon and Lynch. In 1969, Dr. Alfred Whiting, president of Central, spoke at Watts. The next year, a White pastor active in civil rights spoke.

In 1967, women from Watts Street began meeting regularly with women from White Rock Baptist Church in a group they called "Shared Life." The meetings, which started with the goal of understanding each other better in terms of race, continued until 1974. A group of Durham women of both races calling themselves Women in Action began in 1968 and established a center where community members could call with questions during the critical first years of integration in Durham. In Our Separate Ways: Women and the Black Freedom Movement in Durham, North Carolina by historian Christina Green cites the work of the women's groups as one reason Durham was spared some of the violence other cities faced around integration.

Along with the Civil Rights movement, an anti-war movement flourished as the country divided over the Vietnam War. On March 12, 1967, McClernon preached a sermon entitled "Vietnam: A Moral

Crisis."

Dr. Martin Luther King Jr.'s assassination in April 1968 left many reeling and looking for answers to racial violence and turmoil. The deacons' meeting that month captured some of the confusion. "Because the last few weeks have been unusual, confused, fearful, and uncertain, a brainstorming session was called to (consider) what we might do as a congregation toward improving the lot of the disadvantaged of this city. No attempt was made to explore in depth or to find out the feasibility of some twenty suggestions." They passed the suggestions to the mission committee and voted to rescind the race-based, two-tiered membership policy.

In 1969, McClernon joined other clergymen, Black and White, at St. Joseph's AME church to hold a special Vietnam Memorial and worship service. He served on the mayor's committee for opportunities for youth. The committee met at Watts Street. McClernon also worked with the Rev. Julius Corpening of Temple Baptist in the late 60s, lobbying city officials to build a low-income housing unit, according to Corpening's oral history interview.

Watts Street reached out to other Black churches. In 1970, the Carolina Times reported an event with West Durham Baptist Church on Nixon and Athens Street. McClernon "along with the members of WSBC, will bring baskets and eat dinner together at six o'clock, after which the WSBC Minister, Rev. Robert McClernon, will have charge of the service." Watts Street's choir was also part of the service. The Carolina Times also carried ads for a bazaar at Watts Street and the daycare that opened at Watts Street in 1970. Several times in these years, the deacon minutes refer to Bible Studies with other churches, including Black churches.

McClernon would remain a voice for social justice throughout his tenure at Watts Street and beyond.

# # #

McClernon's vision of a better world included many changes within the church. He stressed lay ministry and encouraged deacons to focus on those in their spiritual care. He worked to reshape the church's hierarchy, sharing decision-making beyond the pastor and the deacons.

These efforts were part of a larger change in many Baptist churches. Perhaps reflecting the zeitgeist of the times, decisions about policies and practices, more and more, came to be made by the entire congregation instead of the pastor and the deacons or the pastor alone. By 1970, the SBC had largely adopted a family deacon plan, complete with workbooks to teach deacons how to minister to those in their charge.

McClernon encouraged the deacons to organize geographically, assigning them to individuals in their area. From March through May 1969, he went with a deacon to visit each inactive member of the church to see what the church could do for them. McClernon followed the visits up with a retreat and workshops focused on helping the deacons learn how to minister.

But old habits die hard, and the deacon minutes show repeated attempts by McClernon to get deacons to focus on ministry more than administration. It was a goal not totally reached until 1987, when McClernon was leaving, and the church created a council to handle administration and the deacons became completely a pastoral care group.

In addition to the deacons' role, there were changes in how deacons were selected. They had been a self-perpetuating group. The deacons themselves chose who would succeed them and offered the church a slate of candidates to approve. Congregants were allowed to nominate individuals, but they did not make the final slate without deacon approval.

In October 1965, the church elected its first woman deacon, Delores Atkins, in a process that saw 58 nominations and five ballots in the deacon meeting that determined the slate of candidates. She was ordained in January 1966 and served as the only woman until Beth Upchurch was elected in 1970.

Chris Hamlet, a deacon who was very active in the move to have women deacons, said that as the 1965 election finally wrapped up, another deacon leaned over and said to Hamlet, "You are nothing but a woman-lover!" a charge to which Hamlet happily confessed.

The deacons, with some pushing for change and all wanting to avoid the mayhem of the year before, altered the selection process, and in 1966, members could vote for individual deacons and have at least two choices for each open spot.

When Beth Upchurch joined the deacon board, she wasted no time making her feelings known. The minutes of the January meeting tell us: "Beth Upchurch confronted fellow board members with the 'token' integration which the church practices in the membership of its board of deacons ... she urged its members to become aware of the moving force for good which the women of the church are causing to happen and to consider them as female, whole persons in their own right fully able to serve along with males on the board. The board would need to nominate and to support the election of women if they would desire to change this situation. Members of the board acknowledged the validity of her contention."

From there, the number of women on the deacon board slowly climbed. In 1976, Jean Dula served as chair of the deacons, earning praise for her leadership skills. McClernon "pointed out that many were watching Jean as she is only one of two females that have served as deacon chairperson of Southern Baptist churches."

By 1986, 13 out of 24 deacons were women.

In 1974, the church modified the election process again, creating a church committee to nominate individuals to serve as deacons instead of the deacons doing the nominating. The deacons were allowed to add names to the list of nominees—up to half the number of positions available—if they chose.

Another change was involving the laity in worship. Once a month, a member participated in the service by reading the liturgy or the scripture, a practice that grew steadily over the years. Communion had been served four times a year; McClernon instituted it once a month. When not enough deacons showed up one Sunday morning to serve communion, a system was established so that would not happen again, hopefully. McClernon also created feedback groups, a cross-section of the membership that met with him regularly to help him improve the worship service.

The once proud Sunday evening programs were flagging when McClernon arrived. He instituted a Vespers service at 5:30 on Sunday evenings, followed by a meal from 6 to 6:30 and then a study period for all ages from 6:30 to 7:30. The new program flourished briefly in the months after his arrival, but in April, he wrote in the newsletter: "The following sentence appeared in Contact [newsletter] this past January in reference to our Vesper Service: "We want to keep trying until we are either off of or in the ground." Suffice it to say that Vesper Services will be discontinued after Sunday, April 24. There are clear indications that we require an entirely new approach to our ministry on Sunday evening, including our approach to worship. From a Christian perspective, death must precede resurrection."

The deacons appointed a committee on the life and ministry of the church, and in 1968, the group presented its assessment of life at Watts Street. The congregation could be divided into three groups. "Some are unhappy with the way things are, have difficulty relating to the ministers and fellow church members, and frequently criticize music, curriculum, preaching, trends, etc. This is not an unusual characteristic of Baptist congregations, but the situation is complicated currently by the accelerated pace of social changes and frustrations and anxieties experienced in failure to solve social problems and adjust to change." Then, there is a group of those who are happy with their church. And a third group is steadily falling away.

"In recent years, our Congregation has witnessed declines in the rate of membership growth, attendance at church, financial giving, and active involvement in the programs of the church," the report continued. "Recognition that other congregations have undergone similar experiences and that such declines are part of a general trend in our culture does not diminish our guilt and concern. It is not surprising that members want to know why these things are happening and often assign blame to particular persons or events or decisions in the life of the church."

"The Committee believes that a more valuable approach to our problems would be a concerted effort by the Deacons and all members of the Congregation to discover anew the essence of

Christian faith and the nature and mission of the Christian Church."

The report made suggestions for every area of church life, beginning with revising the church covenant and the rules of order. Missions were reorganized by creating a board of missions to oversee different groups, and evangelism was separated from missions. "Are we now, or do we want to be organized to 'take the gospel out into the world?'" the report questioned, without offering an answer. Again, the idea of a church council was proposed.

McClernon cited a new openness and trust in the church the following year, but in July 1970 he presented a seven-page proposal to reform the church, which included the possibility of breaking into smaller groups or house churches. McClernon wrote that the congregation needed more fellowship and more connection to deal with its differences and to support each other. He proposed boards to oversee missions, education, worship and music, financial stewardship, and institutional support (taking care of the building). He suggested a board to oversee it all, which would include a member from each house church, board, and age group. It is not clear what happened to the report. There is no further mention of it in church archives.

At the deacons' meeting the next year, McClernon tried again. The minutes report: "Mr. McClernon shared his personal feelings with the group in relation to his continuing search for meaning in relationship to his commitment to Christ and how that commitment was exercised in his vocational, family, and personal life. He suggested that most all persons have these same kinds of questions and search for meaning, and asked the Board to join him in the quest for values that would truly reflect commitment to Christ. He suggested that the Board might become a supportive, helping community as participants together continue their Christian growth. He noted that the Board had, in the past, been this kind of group and suggested that members would find more meaning in participation through this kind of community than merely as functionaries in a task-oriented month meeting."

His frustration was again evident at the September 1971 deacons' meeting. The deacons have asked for his thoughts. "I simply no longer believe that our business acumen, our skill in group dynamics, our personal contacts and ability in personal diplomacy, our spokesmanship for various congregational factions, nor an intensified promotional campaign for money or participation will point the people of our church towards a rekindled faith in God and a higher level of joy, peace, and purpose in life." He talked about the responsibility of deacons. "It does not seem likely that we can exercise this responsibility faithfully and make progress toward becoming means for the restoration and renewal of the congregation committed to our care until we give thought to our own relationship to God and the brethren." He said he had no desire to tell individuals or the board what they should do. "But I urge you for your own soul's need, for the sake of this church, for God's sake, do something!"

Reading McClernon's many reports and statements, the urgency of his beliefs comes through. He repeatedly stressed to his congregation that they were living in between times. The old order was passing away and the new world order was taking shape. It was hard to be the church of Jesus Christ in the midst of the struggle. He called on people to discuss issues freely, to call others on their half-truths and lies, and to hold each other in Christian fellowship. Being a Christian in the modern world was not for the faint-hearted, he made clear.

From 1967 to 1973, McClernon had an ally in his sense of urgency in Jim Grant, Watts Streets's first Minister of Education. Before Grant, Watts Street had directors of education, whose job was often combined with office worker. Like McClernon, he had strong ties to the ABC and, at one point, called the congregation "lukewarm" in their faith.

Grant stayed for six years; previously, the longest anyone in charge of education had stayed was three years. He brought in teachers from the ABC headquarters in Valley Forge, Pennsylvania, to train local teachers and established discipleship classes for fifth and sixth graders. He began the tradition of holding Youth Sundays where the young people of the church ran the service, started a breakfast served after the Thanksgiving morning service, and sponsored the church's athletic programs with basketball and softball. He took the youth group to retreats at the ABC facility in Green Lake, Wisconsin, trips fondly remembered by many. At one church meeting, Grant pleaded for more order, saying we didn't need to throw out all the rules in the new freedoms of the 1960s. We need to take attendance in Sunday School, he stressed.

Grant was also an outspoken opponent of the Vietnam War, a feeling not universally shared in the church at the time. After Grant accepted a call to be the senior minister at a church in Elmira, New York, Bob McClernon recalled Grant's tenure:

"We were frequently at odds over the program and materials of our ministry of Christian education. Do you recall the flack filling the sky when some of us discovered the photo of Michaelangelo's statue of young David in the buff, displayed in all his innocent glory on a page in the United Church of Christ study book? And the controversy surrounding the creative, theologically alert, courageous, and brash Jim Grant? Loss of Jim was, I believe without question, the greatest suffered by our church during these years, for under his vigorous (if less than diplomatic) leadership, we were on the way toward a superb ministry of education."

In his end-of-the-year report in 1972, McClernon was proud of the year the church had. The deacon minutes tell us he "expressed good feeling about the year just passed. It is his belief that we have something very special and unique here and that we should be willing and feel obligated to tell people about it and encourage others to come and share it with us." Grant agreed. Grant "feels that this has been the finest year since he has been at Watts Street. He has been pleased with the way people have worked, the programs carried out, etc., but primarily with the feeling tone of the various groups in the church. He feels this is due to the fact that people seem to be enjoying each other and are learning to live together more happily."

Some glimpses of Watts Street life over the years are reflected in these photos.

A hardworking kitchen crew

A choir rehearsal

Girls' Auxiliary Coronation, 1960s

Youth Group performance

# # #

As church members reconsidered relationships within the church, they also reconsidered their relationships with other Baptist groups.

Under Carr's tenure, Watts Street had considered affiliating with the American Baptist Convention and had studied the possibility several times. The disenchantment with the SBC curriculum was but one symptom of the church feeling out of step with some of the SBC's programs. But in July 1964, the church voted not to join the ABC.

The next year, with a new pastor with ABC ties, the issue resurfaced. In August 1966, a committee on joint affiliation presented a report to the congregation, calling for a churchwide discussion and then a vote. They recommended staying with the SBC and joining the ABC beginning in January 1967.

The matter was discussed at length at a church meeting in November. The biggest sticking point was the ABC's membership in the National Council of Churches (NCC), an organization that had been calling for an end to racial segregation for years. There were rumors of communist infiltration into the NCC and charges that the group's support of the Vietnam War was not all that a patriotic citizen would want. A motion was made to join the ABC but disavow the NCC. The motion was defeated, and the congregation voted to join the ABC without qualifications.

That vote apparently did not end the concerns about the NCC, and in 1969, the deacons conducted a study of the Council. The Watts Street report stressed that the NCC was not perfect and not binding on member organizations, but that, on balance, its policies were good ones and that it could accomplish things individual churches could not accomplish on their own. The report recommended more study and discussion.

The ABC was racially diverse, and most of the ABC churches in the South were Black. In 1970, the ABC formed ABCOTS— American Baptist Churches of the South. Watts Street, an all-white church, became a racial minority at its regional meetings. The church sent messengers to both the SBC and the ABC, and McClernon himself alternated, attending one convention one year and the other the next. In 1972, the messengers Watts Streets sent to ABCOTS returned with "overwhelmingly positive" comments on their experiences.

The same could not be said of the church's relationship with its local group, the Yates Baptist Association.

# # #

In September 1961, the Ruth Sunday School class formally asked the deacons to consider not requiring a second Baptism for those who joined the church after being baptized in another denomination. Historically, baptism for Baptists means immersion. The deacons appointed a committee and came to no conclusion. Seven years later, when the committee studying church life made its recommendations, it also suggested that the church consider changing its policy on immersion. Position papers on the wisdom of changing the requirement or keeping it the same were discussed in Sunday School class for three Sundays in January and February of 1969. At the February church meeting, the congregation voted to change church policy to not require a second baptism, 125 to 31.

That was the beginning of a conflict that would challenge Watts Street's relationship with the Yates Baptist Association, a group Watts Street had been part of since Yates's founding in 1948.

In March, as word of Watts Street's decision spread, officials at Yates Baptist Association asked that McClernon come to talk with them about the church's immersion policy. He declined to go alone, and apparently, several church members joined him.

At the annual association meeting that fall, a motion to put Watts Street on watch care—a kind of probation—for a year for "their willful departure from orthodox principles of the Christian religion as taught in the Bible and as believed by Baptists" was voted down in favor of a motion that asked that the Yates Association study the membership policies of all the churches in the association.

The association appointed a committee of five men, who struggled mightily with the serious issues involved. They found eight churches in the association that either did not require baptism by immersion or left the issue murky enough to raise questions. They met 15 times over eight months, distributed and tabulated a lengthy survey, and tried to reconcile Baptist principles of Believer's Baptism and the autonomy of the local church.

Its report, presented at the annual meeting in October 1970, concluded: "In light of the variety of membership practices within the churches of the Yates Baptist Association," no further action be taken against Watts Street or other churches and "with mutual respect for our differences as we continue, as in past years, to do together God's work in the area of our association." They encouraged baptism for members but asked that the consideration of a church's membership policy on immersion not be a criterion for membership in the Yates Baptist Association.

The Yates moderator supported the association's decision, saying the contested immersion policy was not good but not so bad. "After all," he wrote, in a comment that must have rankled at Watts Street, "whether a parent applies the whip or a rebuke to a child depends on how serious the offense is."

But, others did not agree and presented an amendment to the Yates constitution that would require all members of each church to be immersed. The motion garnered much support, with 135 voting for and 94 voting against, but failed to gain the two-thirds majority needed to change the policy.

Back from the Baptist wars, McClernon summed up the relationship with Yates for the deacons, saying that the situation involved more than a debate over immersion. There was a division in the association about how much energy should go into evangelism and how much should go into the work of the Social Ministries Committee. Watts Street was firmly identified with its mission. There were complaints about Watts Street's lack of devotion to Yates's programs. And what was perceived as "the 'superior' attitude of the church toward the Association over the years has created a backlog of animosity now being expressed in membership policy." And McClernon said some ministers in the Association are smarting because the position they took at the last associational meeting was not adopted. "They do not like to lose."

And if all that was not enough, it was reported that a deacon of Watts Street was seen leaving a supermarket with a six-pack of beer.

McClernon praised the church for debating the issue of immersion honestly and referred to "the growing discovery that we can speak with honesty, even with anger, and remain together We can now, if we choose to do so, speak to each other as Christian brothers in a fashion that was not possible twelve months ago."

In July 1971, at the church meeting, McClernon announced that he wanted to "get on with being church" rather than spend so much time on the controversy with Yates. And the records for the next several years show more involvement in activities with Yates.

But the issue would linger and spread. The Baptist State Convention of North Carolina debated and had a vote much like the one Yates had—a motion to amend bylaws to require immersion for all members obtained a majority, but not the two-thirds needed to amend the bylaws. The state convention would repeat the futile vote at least three times.

And Yates and Watts Street would struggle with how to report members. Yates asked for a breakdown in the list of members Watts Street provided, indicating who had been immersed and who had not. Watts Street declined to divide their membership for Yates, insisting that the church had the right to determine its own membership. They did agree that Yates had the right to determine who could serve as a messenger to their meetings.

Yates rejected that compromise.

In 1973, four Watts Street members met with a committee of 11 appointed by the state Baptists to convince Watts Street and a dozen other "differing" churches to change their policy. Watts Street's response was to affirm its policy with another church vote. In 1974, Watts Street made sure to send a full contingent of messengers to the state convention, aware that the convention was considering whether to disfellowship Watts Street and its fellow offenders. No action was taken against Watts Street that year.

The issue seemed to settle into an uneasy resolution; Watts Street never provided divided membership lists, and Yates and the state Baptists did not break fellowship with them. Watts continued to participate in Yates-sponsored activities. Several members of Watts Street were very involved with Yates Village, a living situation being built for seniors of limited incomes. As late as May 1980, deacon notes include a motion that Watts Street did not identify non-immersed members in its reports to Yates.

In 1982, the deacons recorded more discussion about Watts Street's lack of participation with Yates and a disagreement with Yates's mission director. He wanted to build new churches in the area; Watts Street wanted more support for the churches that were already there.

The relationship with Yates would limp along throughout McClernon's tenure. Each year, Watts Street continued to fill out forms for Yates, giving a variety of details about the church. In January 1985, Watts Street received a letter from Yates bringing sad news. "I regret that your church did not make the perfect letter list for 1984. In order that you may be aware of the corrections made to your letter or information that was omitted, I am enclosing a copy of your letter with the errors noted thereon."

Someone wrote "Stick It!" in ink across the top of the letter and dropped it in the files.

# # #

The church's mission programs in these years were often aimed at meeting the needs of the younger generation. In 1966, church members tried to address the need for emergency foster care. With the house the church owned next door at 1022 Urban St. in mind, they approached the county about setting up a shelter for foster care, only to run afoul of zoning laws. Their next attempt was to rent out the property and use the income to fund another shelter. Eventually, they were forced to settle for encouraging church members to become foster parents.

In 1969, the church dropped one of its long-time ministries. They stopped hosting a preschool for developmentally delayed children because the city schools began providing the service. This process of starting a program and then getting support outside of the church and turning it over to the larger community was one that would often be repeated in Watts Street's mission efforts.

It was a time of great worry about youth. A church report that advocated the creation of what became Hassle House gives a vivid picture of what the congregation was worried about.

"We believe that high school-age young people desperately need to have available people with whom they can work through their frustrations; people they can trust and who know how to listen. We believe that, in many ways, the present generation is facing some of the most perplexing and mind-bending problems and decisions ever to weigh down upon the heads of any generation. The Viet Nam War Crisis with the concomitant moral dilemma of having to decide whether to fight in a war held to be unjust and immoral by some young people; The Eco-Crisis; The Nuclear Proliferation Crisis; The growing domestic and worldwide Revolutionary Crisis; The Educational Crisis: The rapidly changing Value-System-Crisis; The Generation-Gap Crisis; the World-Wide Inequality Crisis; etc."

Hassle House, a mission of Watts Street Baptist Church in the house that is now the W. E. Stanley Mission House.

The report went on to say that youth feel powerless. The church proposed to open a gathering place where youth could seek help at

1022 Urban Street. For more than ten years, Hassle House offered aid to anyone who needed it, evolving into a 24-hour crisis center. It got support from Durham County and earned grants for the services and programs it offered over the years. It closed in 1982 when the county chose to stop its funding.

The programs for children and youth were part of many efforts to meet the needs of the moment. The church opened a daycare in September 1970 to support families in need of childcare. Watts Street held its first CROP walk and maintained a food closet for those in need for several years until it was folded into the work done at Urban Ministries. JoNell McClernon and Anne Drennan, both nurses, provided medical care for migrant workers for several summers. In 1978, the church joined DCIA—Durham Congregations in Action. For several years, the church hosted blood drives for the Red Cross. There was a special Watts Street account. In exchange for the church donating 90 pints of blood a year, members were guaranteed a transfusion should they need one. The church offered space for the Dispute Settlement Center. Watts Street members moved to address the needs of the elderly in their neighborhood and worked with other churches to establish Meals on Wheels. The church sponsored several refugee families over the years.

In 1971, McClernon sent out a letter to those in the church older than 50, asking them to join a ministry group for those who had reached retirement age. McClernon, Jenny Lee, and Ann Barbee knocked on doors in the area around Watts Street, asking if there was anyone who would like to meet with them. Several neighbors did join, and a group called the Thursday Trekkers began. They met at the church on Thursday (hence the name) and often heard a speaker and had lunch. Then they branched out, with regular trips planned to the beach, to sightsee, to the malls.

In 1972, the ABC (which that year had become the American Baptist Churches of the USA) established an "associated relationship" with the Church of the Brethren and the congregation sent a message to the North Carolina Church of the Brethren acknowledging the relationship. McClernon and Gene Johnson traveled to Winston- Salem to meet with members of the Church of the Brethren.

By 1973, Watts Street had reached its 50th anniversary. As part of the anniversary program, deacons held gatherings in their homes four Sundays in March, where a moderator led a discussion on the meaning of Christian fellowship and the past and future of the church. Long- time members shared their memories at a church meeting. Reverends Green, Herring and Carr spoke at a service.

There was much to celebrate. The original membership had grown almost tenfold. Watts Street's WMU, founded when the church was founded, had grown from two circles and 69 members to eight circles and 161 members. It had reached its peak in 1962, with 12 circles and 180 members. But as the 60s rolled on and opportunities opened for women elsewhere, membership declined. Many church women became more concerned with local problems and less with foreign missions. In 1968, the Watts Street group was reorganized. Long-time members had mixed feelings, but the new system called for fewer officers and more flexibility. Women could join a mission study group, a mission prayer group, or a mission action. Meetings were scheduled so that members could belong to more than one group.

The church had doubled its property with purchases in 1947 and 1959 and greatly expanded its building by adding the education wing in 1953. In 1969, the church had completed a remodel of the sanctuary to accommodate a massive new pipe organ, replacing the one given in honor of Mary Lyon forty years earlier.

McClernon praised the congregation, saying that people were more interested in the gospel and what it means personally. "Some of us are having second thoughts about having thrown the Gospel baby out with the fundamentalist bath water." People are kinder to each other and more willing to do the work of the church with less criticism, he said.

As part of the 50th anniversary, the church held its first Moravian love feast, which would become a beloved tradition for the next fifty years. Mary Ann Stone initiated the service and provided leadership for its first 15 years. Chrismons—decorations in silver and gold that carry a religious message—were also introduced for the 50th anniversary, and each year since then Watts Street has a

Christmas tree, set to the left in the sanctuary, covered with beautiful ornaments.

Preparing for the love feast.

Clark Cahow wrote a church history for the occasion. He wrote of the church's recent past. "The younger generation was becoming disenchanted with the institutionalized church, racial tension was reaching its explosive peak, and the nation was involved in a war that could not be justified, could not be won, but could only divide and sap the nation spiritually, emotionally, and politically. Whether we liked it or not, change was upon us."

But Watts Street had met the moment, he said. "The history of WSBC is a history of a church in crisis from its very beginning, and yet we have thrived. We were organized as a family church. Although our membership is dispersed throughout the city and county, we are still a family church. In fifty years, the town of Durham has become a city, and the city limits have moved far to the North and the West. In many respects, however, the church has remained "on the edge of town"—the cutting edge—a leader in the spiritual and secular affairs of our city."

In 1973, there was a sense that Watts Street had weathered the storm and a promising future was beckoning.

A gathering of Watts Street pastors and their wives for the church's 50th anniversary in 1973. From left to right: Ethel and Owen Herring, JoNell and Bob McClernon, Mary and Slyvester Green, and Martha and Warren Carr.

# # #

With half a century behind them, the congregation continued its ministries. The gas crisis threatened to hamper the youth group's trips, but they rented a bus and went on. Louise Ham donated $3000 to make a library in her late husband's honor. The deacons continued to struggle with their role. Ken Harrell, the minister of music who arrived in 1970 and would stay 27 years, directed the chancel choir in Mass in Time of War by Haydn—long considered to contain an anti- war sentiment, in 1974. The church worked on summer recreation programs for housing projects. Efforts at forming relationships with the Black community in Durham continued, while

Watts Street remained an all-white church.

The church decided to get out of the parsonage business and sold the McClernon family the house they were living in, replacing a parsonage with a housing allowance.

Earlier efforts to streamline serving communion had not proved totally successful and there was discussion that the deacons needed to line up in a more orderly fashion. There were a few Sundays when not enough deacons showed up to serve communion, leading to a scramble. There was another unsuccessful attempt to get the unruly congregation to enter the sanctuary reverently and quietly.

In 1977, Watts Street held its first bazaar, which would grow into an annual event. The WMU Circle 3 gradually morphed into "the bazaar ladies" —a nickname they delighted in. They would meet on Monday mornings at the church throughout the year to make beautiful crafts to sell at the bazaar in November. They allocated ten percent of their proceeds to the church's missions and the rest to improvements in the church building. The bazaar ladies, following a proud tradition of women's fund-raising in churches, made the decisions about where the money they raised would be spent. Projects over the years have included improvements to staff offices, the nursery, the kitchen, and many places in the building. They refurbished the ladies' parlor—now a chapel—and provided the parquet floor in the sanctuary, and purchased a sound system including receivers for the hard of hearing.

When it was time in 1978 to look for a new Minister of Education, frustration was expressed with the closed nature of the selection process. This time, a search committee was created, including members of the congregation, and the result was the Rev. Richard Chorley, who served as minister of education until 2002 and was much loved by the congregation.

# # #

As the congregation at Watts Street continued to work on being church to each other and in the world, the SBC was in turmoil. At the 1979 convention in Houston, the Southern Baptist messengers elected a fundamentalist, Adrian Rogers, as president. The conflict between the moderates and the fundamentalists in the convention had always been present, but from 1979 onward, the fundamentalists would have the upper hand. The loss to those who had grown up in a moderate Baptist tradition that was rapidly disappearing was profound.

In 1980, the SBC elected Bailey Smith as President. He announced that "God Almighty does not hear the prayers of a Jew," and Watts Street adopted two resolutions in response, one calling for tolerance and the other for Smith's resignation. Two years later, after the convention in Pittsburgh, Watts Street's messengers returned with hope for reconciliation, saying a spirit of tolerance had prevailed. That spirit had disappeared the next year at the 1984 meeting in Kansas City, where the fundamentalists consolidated their power and passed a resolution against ordaining women. Watts Street's messengers returned dejected. And so it would go for years. Always, the possibility of withdrawing was discussed. Year after year, the decision was made to stay and try to influence the outcome.

With the national organization in the hands of the fundamentalists, the Baptist State Convention of North Carolina hung in the balance for several years, making a serious effort to balance the moderate and fundamental wings of the denomination. Southeastern Seminary in Wake Forest would become a theological battleground in the 1980s.

In 1986, the Home Mission Board of the Southern Baptist Convention announced it would give no financial aid to churches with women pastors. The Baptist State Convention of North Carolina, which in 1975 had adopted a resolution supporting women called to be deacons and pastors, asked the SBC to reconsider. The decision to not fund women pastors, according to Watts Street, "supports the theologically abhorrent teaching that by nature women are unfit for ordination. It is furthermore a clear hindrance to the full exercise of the historic Baptist principle of the rights of each local church to call whomever it will, regardless of gender, to the pastorate or other professional role." Watts Street began directing some of its contributions to more moderate groups.

None of these ongoing issues would be resolved in McClernon's tenure.

Within Watts Street, McClernon often mentioned his concerns about declining membership. In 1975, he told the deacons that people were not joining Watts Street like they were joining other places, and only three children were baptized at Watts Street that year. In 1977, he suggested, "It is time to think about being graciously aggressive in working to maintain our membership." In 1978, he said, "Twenty-five years ago, we were a Baptist congregation with a highly distinctive character, one which gave us few competitors. Were we to investigate, we might discover that today, others have caught up with us, giving people far more options for church membership from which to choose." The church listed 1,332 members when McClernon became pastor and had gradually declined to 1,062 when he departed.

# # #

As Watts Street moved through the 1980s, the congregation continued to experiment with new ways of being the church in the world and with aspects of the worship service. In 1981, dance was incorporated into a worship service and one of the dancers—a plump man in a small leotard—had a wardrobe malfunction. McClernon fielded a flood of complaints from church members. It was the last time dancers appeared as part of the service in McClernon's tenure.

In 1982 Dick Chorley began the tradition of an all-church weekend at Fort Caswell called the All Ages Beach Retreat. Eleanor Whitfield retired as church secretary after 35 years of service—the longest-serving staff member at Watts Street ever. The church sponsored scouting troops for boys and girls and basketball teams at the YMCA. A Family Worship Retreat was held at Camp Caraway. The church had a softball team. One year, the youth challenged the deacons to a game. The deacons accepted the challenge but failed to record the score. There is mention of a Women's Christian Bowling league. Security remained a concern. The building was robbed several times, and a security committee was appointed, selecting 4 to 6 men to police the church building after incidents of strangers roaming the church halls during the worship service.

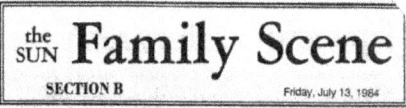

the SUN Family Scene

SECTION B   Friday, July 13, 1984

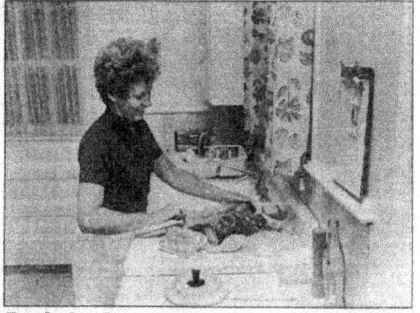

Ready for dinner guests

Liz Lutz, a volunteer host at a church-spon-
sored shelter for homeless women, prepares   dinner for her guests.
                                                  Sun staff photo by Kevin Keister

Hosts volunteer the hospitality

Liz and Worth Lutz are the volunteer hosts on a recent evening
at the shelter for homeless
women.
   Mrs. Lutz arrives there at about
5:30 p.m. She checks the log book
to see who is expected, and
whether there are notes on any
special needs of the guests. She
finds the menu, which is planned
weekly by a volunteer nutrition-
ist. Next she checks the refrigera-
tor for leftovers that could be

fresh sliced vegetables await the
diners. Tall glasses of iced tea
and milk stand at the place set-
tings.
   In the brief "grace" that is said,
Mr. Lutz gives thanks for each of
the guests by name, and there is a
feeling of well-being as the plates
are passed.
   Guests talk a little about what
they've done that day. They volunteer information about themselves as they wish, but aren't

Hosts learn certain unwritten
rules that have to do with their
guests' lifestyles. "You start asking questions from the last time
you saw them," she says, but even
learn not to to that, because,
"Nothing is definite in their
lives."
   Hosts are not supposed to be
counselors, or even to solicit personal information, she points out.
"All this is is a refuge, a space
that's theirs because they don't

In an ambitious mission effort, Watts Street ran a shelter for homeless women in the house at 1024 Urban Avenue. From 1984 to 1988, Watts Street operated a shelter for homeless women in the house behind the church, previously home to Hassle House. Church members held meetings with neighborhood leaders who were concerned about a homeless shelter opening in the neighborhood. Flora Stanley provided money to refurbish the house. It was named the W. E. Stanley Mission House in honor of her late husband, who had served as the Superintendent of Sunday School at Watts Street for many years.

At that time, there was no city shelter for women, few for men, and none for families. The project began when one church member found someone sleeping under the stairwell in a rental they owned. It was a strictly Watts Street operation: the church provided the place, the staff, and most of the volunteers. The shelter needed two shifts of volunteers each day, a dinner shift from 5 to 8 p.m. and an overnight shift. It was a struggle to get enough volunteers. The coordinators were Sally Browder, Anne Drennan, Doris Cooper McCoy, and Fred Starr. The shelter closed with the founding of Genesis House, a shelter for women, children, and families. Jim Drennan recalled that it was exhausting running a 365-day-a-year shelter. "We patched it together, but it was hard," he said, adding that the church learned about its limitations and about what it means to provide hospitality.

The mission house has been used frequently since then as part of Host Homes, another program that started as a Watts Street mission, offering shelter for patients and families in Durham for treatment at Duke Hospital.

Baby dedications were done at Watts Street during McClernon's tenure —a practice Carr had scorned. In the fall of 1984, an unusual dedication service occurred, one that McClernon wrote especially for the family and the deacons approved unanimously. It was for Benjamin Rumer, son of member Dick Rumer, and his wife, Barbara Rumer. What was unusual about it was that Barbara was Jewish and, at that time, intended to remain so. Over the years, the Rumers raised three children in the church, and both parents remain active in the work of the church at this writing.

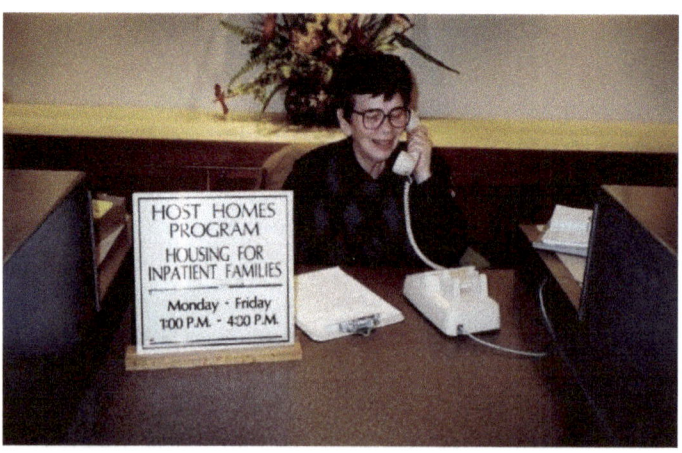

Christine Stocks working at a program she helped to create, Host Homes.

Watts Street's Board of Missions supported the creation of Threshold, a clubhouse where mentally challenged individuals could be trained in work and social skills. It opened in 1985 after many years of work by Shirley Strobel and others at Watts Street.

In 1985, handicap ramps were added to the entrances to the

church, a gift from the Hare family. The possibility of an elevator was discussed. The church also adopted the notion of long-range planning that year and appointed a committee.

In 1986, Watts Street, at the urging of the Yates' Association, agreed to host a revival from March 16 to 18, 1986. It began with McClernon offering the congregation a history of revivals in North America, going all the way back to Jonathan Edwards' "Sinners in the Hands of an Angry God." The Wednesday before the revival began, the church held a prayer service for the revival's success that included a supper of soup and sandwiches. They passed on the fire and brimstone, inviting three preachers not known for their conservative views. They were Haywood Holderness, pastor at Westminster Presbyterian Church in Durham; William Finlator, senior pastor at Pullen Memorial Baptist Church; and Lisa Grabarek Matthews, a Yale Divinity School graduate who grew up at Watts Street and had been ordained there.

The long-range planning committee released its report the next month, April 1986. It said the church had "held its own" for the past two decades, like many in the Yates Association. It was not a time of great growth in membership, but they had not lost ground. In less tangible measures, church members were very happy. "Worship, the freedom to explore new ideas and what it means to be a Christian, and fellowship received high marks on a survey completed by 82 individuals.... To a somewhat lesser extent, Christian education and music were listed as positives." A decided lack of evangelism was noted.

"When asked to respond to the question of possible new or continuing ministries, members cited shelter, urban ministry, and Habitat at the top of the list," the committee reported. A goal was set to increase the level of financial support for missions until one-third of the operating budget was allocated to outreach projects (including in-kind contributions) by 1990. Improving relations with the Soviet Union was listed as a concern and would bear fruit in upcoming years in a relationship with a Baptist church in Kostroma, Russia. The report also put numbers to their goals, wanting eight new members by 1990 and seeking a contribution of five percent of the taxable income from each household.

The support for Habitat was not a surprise. Watts Street had wholeheartedly embraced Habitat for Humanity, a nonprofit started out of Koinonia Farms in 1976 with the goal of eliminating homelessness. Volunteers built homes, and Habitat then sold them to low-income families for the cost of the materials. In 1983, four adults and six youths from Watts Street traveled to Oak Ridge, Tennessee, to work on a Habitat project. They returned the next two summers, and with the leadership of Worth Lutz and Dick Chorley, a Durham chapter was established in 1985, building hundreds of homes in Durham. The same year, 1985, the church pledged to raise $60,000 over the next three years to expand mission programs, including Habitat.

The long-range report also considered, again, rewriting the church covenant, and the decision, a long time coming, was made to move to a church council form of government, freeing the deacons to work on lay ministry exclusively. The deacons decided to train several members in the Stephen Ministry, an intensive program of lay ministry to those in crisis. Six people attended a 12-day course in Baltimore. Another proposal from the committee was aimed at the men of the church. The women of the church were organized and active; the deacons sought to create a group of Watts Street men. (This had been a concern from the beginning. While the women of the church had been organized from the beginning in the WMU, the men of the church never created a "Brotherhood"—a group many Baptist churches included and one that the Yates membership form asked about year after year. While men at the church took on many mission projects over the years, a formal brotherhood was never to be.)

An early Habitat for Humanity group.

In 1987, the SBC met in St. Louis. Moderates in the organization were asked to relinquish their positions of responsibility in the convention and Pat Robertson, conservative evangelist and presidential candidate, spoke at the convention. Watts Street's messengers returned discouraged. A new group of Baptists disillusioned with the SBC was forming that year. McClernon questioned whether anyone needed another group of Baptists and said the church could find everything it wanted in the ABCUSA. The congregation voted to join the Southern Baptist Alliance (which later became the Alliance of Baptists) anyway.

Throughout these years, McClernon counseled individuals at church. The 75th history says some members believe the greatest contribution McClernon made to their lives was not in church activities but in one-on-one counseling sessions. He also spent time volunteering with the mentally ill at John Umstead State Hospital in Butner. Long-time members report that McClernon had deep compassion for the mentally ill. For several years, he had considered leaving Watts Street to earn an MA in social work at UNC-Chapel Hill and get a job working with the mentally ill, but the church had asked him to remain until the long-range plan was finished. Umstead offered him a job without requiring him to earn a degree, and he announced his resignation in April 1987.

Throughout his years at Watts Street, McClernon led many study groups and stressed that the life of faith was a journey with many unknown twists and turns. Jim Drennan said McClernon was "part preacher, part poet." McClernon wrote new lyrics for some familiar tunes, and the church gathered them into a supplemental hymnal. "He introduced me to Rabbi Heschel and Frederick Buechner, among others. My unpacking of the old-time substitutionary atonement I had grown up with came at Bob's sermons. I also was privileged to be in a breakfast book club he managed using a book called The Seasons of a Man's Life. I learned a lot," Drennan said.

The McClernons said their farewells at a reception in August. In a newspaper interview for his departure, McClernon praised the Watts Street congregation. The church had accomplished so much because of the work of the people. His job was to be the coach, he said. His emphasis on mission and social action had become part of the church's DNA. The bulletin for his last Sunday read, "We embarked on a journey of 22 years with this dedicated man as our pilot. The way has not been a smooth one, but Bob's piercing honesty has strengthened us and moved us as individuals and as a congregation to take the Christian stance on many difficult issues."

Dr. John Eddins, a professor at Southeastern, agreed to serve as interim. Dr. Bob Dale, also of Southeastern, agreed to work with the search committee. The congregation considered where they were and where they wanted to go and began to look for their next pastor.

For peace, like war, must be waged.

Rev. Mel Williams

The Mel Williams
Years, 1988 to 2012

The Reverend T. Melvin Williams, with his wife, Jan Adams Williams, and young children Jenna and Mark, arrived in Durham in July 1988. They arrived in his bright yellow Volkswagen Bug, a car a newspaper reporter described as "delightfully tacky." Williams is a North Carolina native who grew up in Aberdeen and attended Wake Forest College before studying at Yale University's Divinity School. He served for ten years at Pullen Memorial Baptist Church as an associate under the leadership of the Reverend William Finlator, an outspoken opponent of the war in Vietnam and segregation.

Mel and Jan Williams with Jenna and Mark.

Williams came to Durham after eight years at Oakhurst Baptist Church in Decatur, Georgia, near Atlanta. Oakhurst was a neighborhood in transition, and the church population diversified with the neighborhood and became active in many progressive Baptist causes. Walker Knight, a respected journalist and a member at Oakhurst, began publishing SBC Today, an independent newspaper that challenged the fundamentalists dominating the SBC, out of Oakhurst in 1983. SEEDS, a magazine focusing on hunger, began at Oakhurst. Members founded Café 458, a restaurant for the homeless, along with providing overnight lodging in the Sunday School rooms. Members were also involved with Christians Against Hunger and the Southern Prison Ministry Group. Williams said he was warned that he might find Watts Street "a little button-downed" for him.

His goals at Watts Street were to be a good pastor and, to meet the needs of the church community, and to "bring a prophetic challenge," especially around racism, poverty, and gun violence. "Following Jesus means doing what he said and did—compassion for everyone and a commitment to 'good news for the poor' (Luke 4 and Matthew 25) and a life of nonviolence: 'would that they knew the things that make for peace' (Luke 19:41)," Williams recalled.

When Williams arrived, several major changes were underway at Watts Street. The move to a church council took effect that fall. The long process of disengagement with the SBC was underway, although Watts Street would not formally leave until a decade later. The month before Williams arrived, the church voted to support a freeze on nuclear weapons. Watts Street had established a reputation as a church focused on mission and social justice issues, and Williams was ready to expand on it.

"My emphasis was going to be missions," Williams recalled. "How can we get outside of our walls? The church has to go to where the need is." He described Watts Street as a compassionate community that tried to meet the moment. "We are a Biblical people." He stressed three principles throughout his time at Watts Street: every member is a minister, the church exists for the sake of those who are not in it, and there is no issue that is too controversial for the church to face.

By February 1989, Williams had met with all of the deacon groups, providing an opportunity for all members to speak with him. The church began to have regular Wednesday night suppers every second Wednesday. In April 1989, the church hosted a Seder meal led by Rabbi John Friedman and arranged by Barbara Rumer. That year also saw the creation of the church's first computer committee—the beginning of the new technology that would grow in importance over the years.

Williams introduced Watts Street to "sounding the call." It was a practice that began at the Church of the Savior in Washington, D.C., where a member of the church would address the congregation from the pulpit about an issue concerning them, inviting others to meet them at the piano after the service to consider forming a mission group to address the issue. Williams said sound the call was about releasing the congregation's energies for direct involvement in a mission initiative. "The person sounding the call needs to answer the 3 questions. 1. Is this mission good news? 2. Does it seem impossible to accomplish? 3. Is there a good chance we will fail?" Williams said. If the answer to all three questions is yes, "that is a sign that the Spirit is leading us to undertake the mission." A mission group would then be formed, usually of 6 -10 people who would meet regularly to set strategy for the mission with backing from the WSBC Missions Committee.

Many important ministries began in this way during Williams' time at Watts Street, including the Creation Care Ministry, work with AIDS patients, and a long-standing relationship with Iglesia Bautista Emmanuel in San Salvador, El Salvador. In 1991, a call was sounded that led to the creation of One World Market, which sold craft items from low-income workers around the world. Jan Adams Williams was one of the founders and has devoted herself to its success. Rev. Williams described it as "Jan's third child." It has grown from a Christmas shop in the Watts Street Fellowship Hall to a brick-and- mortar store that operates year-round. In 2019, One World Market changed its name to Bull City Fair Trade, and it continues to thrive, selling items from all over the world and supporting many important causes.

***The Rev. Mel Williams with Pastor Miguel Tomas Castro Garcia of
Iglesia Bautista Emmanuel in San Salvador, El Salvador.***

In the fall of 1989, Debbie McGill sounded a call to anyone
interested in forming a sister church relationship with First Calvary
Baptist Church. The pastor at the time was Paul Jackson, a friend of
Williams. For four years, members of the two congregations met
monthly, working at building relationships across the color line. A
joint service was held annually, and the pastors exchanged pulpits.
When Jackson left and a new pastor came, First Calvary discontinued
the relationship.

On the same Sunday that McGill sounded the call for a
relationship with First Calvary, Watts Street gained its first Black
member, Steve Arrington. Now a lawyer in Greensboro, he
remembers that morning well. He was very moved by McGill's
comments, and "I felt a huge push inside me to go down the aisle," he
recalled. He was well aware that he would be the church's first Black
member.

Arrington had started attending Watts Street at the invitation of a
high school friend, Kevin Chorley, son of Rev. Dick Chorley. He was
20 years old and not sure what the future might hold. "It was the right

decision at the right time. Watts Street was the right church. Watts Street is still my spiritual home," he said.

At Watts Street, he said, "no one ever asked me to divorce my intellectual side from my spiritual side." He was aware that he made some people uncomfortable, but most members were very accepting. He was perceived as Steve, an individual, not the first Black member. He stayed for two years, worked with the youth group, and then went on to college at Guilford. He considered a career in the ministry but decided on law school. He specializes in Elder Law. He is married with two sons. He keeps up with several members and visits occasionally. He has never found another church home.

Arrington is proud of his role in Watts Street history. Although a small number of current Watts Street members add valued diversity in race and ethnicity, Watts Street remains a predominantly White church.

# # #

Williams's involvement in the Durham community was a vital part of his ministry. In 1992, he served as president of Durham Congregations in Action, a coalition of over 50 congregations. He began to get more involved when Leslie Dunbar, a member of WSBC and a civil rights activist, asked Williams, "Would you help me organize the Durham faith community to help stop handgun violence?" That request led to the origin of the Religious Coalition for a Nonviolent Durham, which has continued for more than 30 years, organizing vigils at the site of every violent death in Durham, a reentry ministry for ex-offenders, and more recently, a restorative justice mission. Williams said, "Les Dunbar was a mentor for me; and through his influence, we were also able to secure notable civil rights leaders to preach at our annual MLK Sunday service—such as Congressman John Lewis, Vernon Jordan, Will Campbell, and Samuel DuBois Cook."

Williams tackled serious issues of the day in his sermons, always applying the gospel. When the city and county schools combined in 1992, an event that stirred racial fears in some, Williams addressed the change from the pulpit, saying he was preaching about it because it was about fear and fear was a spiritual issue. He was fierce in his opposition to violence, prejudice, and poverty. He told his congregation again and again that the way to deal with the great problems and injustices of the world was to grab hold of the nearest corner and work locally. He preached on relationships—with God and with each other. He preached about what it means to be a Christian in the modern world and what it means to be a Christian community. He preached on joy and sorrow and on God's redeeming love. He delivered many a call to action. Throughout his 24 years at Watts Street, Williams estimated that he preached over 900 sermons.

His sermons were not always totally fierce. Williams, a serious musician, has a lovely tenor voice. He would often break into song during his sermons. One sermon fondly remembered was his tomato sandwich sermon, in which he described making a tomato sandwich and eating it over the sink and thinking of the goodness of God as the juices dripped down his chin. He did several reprises, including one where his father provided tomatoes from his garden for all the members of the congregation.

# # #

One of the hopes when Williams was called to Watts Street was that he would increase membership, particularly among younger families. The church's membership had remained steady through the 1980s, hovering at about 1,000 members at a time when Durham's population was growing rapidly. Roughly 30 new members joined each year in Williams's first years.

The growth in membership was unsettling for some. Williams brought up the topic at the July 1991 deacon meeting, saying that although no one had spoken with him directly, he had heard that "having many new members join the church causes an uneasy feeling on the part of older members." He stressed that "No one wants to see a 'new church' develop alongside the present one" and suggested that he hold office hours where anyone could drop by and talk with him. Talk can bring reconciliation and tolerance, he said. He also offered to hold meetings with members in his home. "A chief problem is how to bring the reality of the situation and perceptions about it together," the minutes read. "In a church like ours with so much variety in membership, there is a wide range of ideas; we can't please everybody, but we need to agree on which aspects of our beliefs are matters of principle."

(It is worth pausing here for a moment to consider membership number. The roughly 1,000 listed on the membership role is questionable. Williams said he used to consider that we had about 500 members "that we could find" and about 300 active members. Others say Baptists are notorious for being flexible in their keeping of membership records.)

The church gradually made progress in uniting all its membership. In a survey in 1990, 58 percent of the congregation said they "definitely fit" at Watts Street. Three years later, it was 65 percent. The survey also identified the need for a children's minister. New members often came with babies and children. The Reverend Diane Eubanks Hill, a Watts Street member and an ordained minister who had worked with the Alliance of Baptists and various churches in North Carolina, became the Minister to Children and Their Families in September 1992. Her importance in connecting young families to the church can hardly be overstated. Hill would remain on staff for 26 years, ministering to and with all ages. Her gifts for connection, pastoral care, administration, worship leadership, and much more wove their way into the life of the congregation in countless ways.

Throughout these years, the deacons and the church council were still defining their roles. It took a bit of sorting out as to which group would have which responsibility. The church council had been approved for a one-year trial in 1988. At a church meeting the next year, the congregation voted to make it permanent. In 1990, in their role of connecting with the congregation and providing opportunities for fellowship, the deacons hosted Epiphany suppers and were pleased with the results. Their minutes record that they were responsible for maintaining connections with their deacon groups but would not "be invading the prerogative of the pastor." They are also divided into four service groups: Denominational Relations, Fellowship, Lay Pastoral Care, and New Members. The Stephen Ministry training group became inactive, the minutes reported. A children's retreat was held, with 25 children attending, with great success.

In August 1990, Iraqi forces under Saddam Hussein invaded Kuwait. International outrage followed, with the United Nations setting a deadline for Iraq to withdraw from Kuwait. The deadline passed with no movement. On January 16, 1991, U.S. and UN troops attacked, forcing Iraqi troops out of Kuwait by the end of February. At Watts Street, the congregation was divided, with some members believing the United States had to act and others believing that war was never the answer. Williams was firmly in the anti-war camp and not one to shy away from difficult subjects.

In 1992, the church began a bereavement committee. Those willing to provide food comfort and plan and host a reception if desired were organized into groups to cover each month. In the wake of one memorable December, where there were three big funeral receptions required in the weeks before Christmas, the ministry changed to a rotating schedule. This work has continued up to the present.

Also in 1992, there were three break-ins at the church in 30 days. The long-awaited mission trip to Durham's sister city, Kostroma, Russia, took place while another mission group headed to Venezuela. Work began on some much-needed kitchen renovations. Each year, the congregation enjoyed a churchwide picnic at the farm of Worth and Liz Lutz.

# # #

Meanwhile, the Baptist Wars continued unabated. Within Watts Street, the struggle over whether to leave a vastly changed SBC continued.

A church night report entitled "This Troubling Time" in February 1989 read, "Those of us who love the convention and have given years of faithful service to it are now disenfranchised." After much discussion throughout the year, the congregation decided to stay with the state Baptists and Yates and join the Southern Baptist Alliance, soon to drop the "Southern" and become the Alliance of Baptists. There was support for a new seminary in Richmond.

Down the road in Wake Forest, North Carolina, the fundamentalist/moderate split was playing out dramatically and painfully. In 1987, a more conservative board of trustees took over at Southeastern Baptist Theological Seminary. Upheaval followed, and four years later, it was estimated that the seminary had lost half its faculty and half its student body and much of its funding. The struggle was followed closely at Watts Street, which had many ties to the seminary. Some who left Southeastern joined Watts Street, describing themselves as refugees.

When Williams had first arrived at Watts Street, the dean at Duke Divinity School asked him to chair a committee considering establishing Baptist Studies at Duke. Williams agreed, and six years later the Baptist House of Studies was established at Duke, with Furman Hewitt, a former Southeastern professor and Watts Street member, as its first director.

Watts Street struggled to maintain its dual affiliation. In 1989, Williams attended the ABC meeting in Milwaukee, and the church sent messengers to the SBC meeting in Las Vegas. When President George H. W. Bush appointed the Rev. Paul Pressler as his ethics advisor, Watts Street sent a letter in protest. Pressler was a leader in the fundamentalist takeover of the SBC and, at this writing, is facing lawsuits stemming from alleged sexual assaults on young men.

In a controversial move in 1990, the church voted to halve its contribution to Yates from $2,000 to $1,000. The next church meeting included a letter from Chris Hamlet about his concern that Watts Street was making decisions rapidly, with little or no study of where the money was going or where it was going to come from in the budget. He was particularly dissatisfied with halving the contribution to Yates, saying it was based on conversations that were hard to pin down. "I am most concerned about the statement in the minutes regarding 'others being dissatisfied with the apparent attitude of the Yates Association toward this congregation.' From personal observation and experience, I am inclined to believe that the attitude of the Yates Association toward this congregation is more to be approved than the attitude of this congregation toward the Association. Until 1946, Watts Street was a typical Southern Baptist Church: then Warren Carr began the process of moving this congregation to the cutting edge of the Christian Church, in the Yates Association, in Durham, and in more distant places. And Bob

McClernon picked up where Warren left off. During these forty-plus years tensions have arisen around events such as the tentative opening of our doors to black people in 1954, the ordination of Addie Davis, and the change in our membership policy Through it all, our friends in the Association have stood by us."

The Yates contribution was restored to $2,000.

The reports from the SBC in New Orleans in 1990 brought no good news for Watts Street. Clarence Whitfield, a Watts Street messenger to the convention, wrote: "The prevailing feeling seemed to me to be one, not only of defeat for the moderate point of view but, of a complete intolerance for any views not consistent with those of the conservatives in charge of the convention."

Watts Street reiterated that it was and would remain a Baptist Church. It cut its contribution to the SBC to the minimum, increased its funds to the ABCUSA, continued its support of the NC Baptists, and continued with the Alliance of Baptists.

In 1991, Watts Street did not send a formal group of messengers to the SBC and joined the Cooperative Baptist Fellowship, a newly formed group within the SBC to represent more moderate Baptists.

Seven more years of consideration of options, weighing of tradition vs. values, and turmoil would take place before Watts Street left the SBC. In 1998, when the SBC announced that wives should "graciously submit" to their husbands, even the most devoted Southern Baptists in the congregation had had enough. It was time to go.

Our formal statement, adopted on October 4, read: "Out of our Baptist heritage and its basis in the authority of scripture, we recognize that WSBC does not ascribe to many of the principles espoused by current SBC leadership. Therefore, with a sense of regret and loss, we find it necessary to formally dissociate our church from the SBC and to delete all references to the SBC from the Rules of Church Order/Church Bylaws."

# # #

Seeking a way to minister to the Durham community, Williams

began meeting with pastors from a nearby neighborhood in 1995. He met with three Black Baptist pastors—from St. John's Missionary Baptist, Northside Baptist, and St. James Baptist—and one White Presbyterian pastor from Blacknall Memorial Presbyterian Church once a month for prayer and Bible study. Whenever he pressed the issue of doing something, the pastors would tell him it was not time yet. They would say they had seen white folks come through their neighborhood before, and then they were gone. They were interested in a long-term relationship, not a one-off. "They taught me patience," Williams recalled. Building relationships takes time. The pastors continued to meet and held a joint worship service at Baldwin Auditorium on Duke's East Campus.

Three years later, Walltown Neighborhood Ministries was established, with all five churches as founding members. The next year, 1999, the Duke Endowment asked the group to apply for a pilot grant. The effort grew into a multi-faceted ministry, including refurbishing a former school as a community center, tutoring for students, job training, summer camps, and neighborhood parties. Watts Street was part of a plan to purchase a house in Walltown so that divinity students might live in and minister to the neighborhood. Habitat for Humanity and the Self-Help Credit Union were among the groups in the area working towards greater home ownership and redevelopment of property. The *Herald-Sun*, in a series of articles in 2000, said the neighborhood "has undergone one of the most impressive turnarounds ever seen in the Bull City." Walltown Ministries celebrated its 25th anniversary recently.

#

In 1997, Music Minister Ken Harrell retired after 27 years at Watts Street. Many members of the church donated funds towards new Chalice hymnals in honor of Harrell. Harrell had directed the choir and played the organ simultaneously—a challenging combination. It took two people to replace him. Larry Speakman began as the new music director, and Tom Bloom became the organist.

Also that year, a major renovation began, which included adding an elevator at the rear entrance to the church. After a long process and much consideration, a new church covenant was adopted.

In 1998, the church celebrated its 75th anniversary with a homecoming dinner at Watts School, where it all began. Warner Ragsdale and Shirly Strobel wrote a history stressing that Watts Street has stayed "on the edge—the cutting edge—a leader in the spiritual and secular affairs of Durham." Watts Street, they wrote, is a religious community "where the college professor and the anti-intellectual, the businessman and the blue-collar worker are able to find each other in Christian comradeship and covenant ethics."

The next years brought a Parish Nurse Ministry, with Anne Drennan serving as a parish nurse, another long-range planning committee, a revivals and renewal committee, and the creation of The Heritage Room, thanks to an anonymous gift of $20,000 and the tireless work of Emily Joiner. The church continued to focus on race. John Hope Franklin spoke at Watts Street in March 1999 on racial reconciliation. In 2001, the church, at the urging of the Peace and Reconciliation Committee, called for a three-year moratorium on the death penalty. The same year, the deacons established a prayer ministry.

Attendance at Watts Street's early worship service, which was started to accommodate the overflow crowds of the 1950s and 1960s, had dwindled greatly, and the service was discontinued in 2004. The next year, Watts Street joined CAN—Congregations and Neighborhoods—a community-wide mission group. In 2006, the church adopted a policy requiring training and background checks for those in the church who worked with children and hired Michelle Old as a childcare coordinator. In 2009, the church ended its contract with the daycare it had housed since 1970.

#

On September 11, 2001, Watts Street was stunned, along with the rest of the nation, when terrorists flew airplanes into the World Trade Center and the Pentagon, killing almost 3,000 people. Williams's sermon the next Sunday was called "Weeping Towards Peace." The scriptures quoted on the front of the bulletin were: "O God, make haste to help us" (Psalm 70:1); "The Lord is near to the brokenhearted, and saves the crushed in spirit" (Psalm 34:18); "Wait for the Lord; be strong and let your heart take courage" (Psalm 27:14); "Seek peace and pursue it" (Psalm 34:14).

As the scope of the tragedy began to register, Americans prayed, lamented, and raged. Diana Jackson, who over the years has made many banners for the church, made one that read, "We pray for comfort, mercy, pardon, awareness, humility, grace. Amen." The Peace and Reconciliation Committee drafted a statement against further violence and encouraged individuals to contact elected officials and media with concerns about United States plans to go after terrorists by invading Afghanistan.

A youth Sunday with Amanda McCoy, Beth Toler (intern with youth), Michael Day, the Rev. Dick Chorley, and Mary Elizabeth Hill.

Dick Chorley retired in 2002. An agenda item on the Adult Education Committee's next meeting put it plainly. "Will we have problems functioning after Dick retires?" Clearly, there would be challenges. Chorley had worked at Watts Street for 23 years. His legacy includes the All Ages Beach Retreat, Habitat for Humanity beginning in Durham, work for the Kostruma partnership, Men's Breakfast, Lenten small groups and so much more. He had been a central part of the faith journey of many Watts Streeters over decades. With Chorley's retirement came major changes in the church staffing. Hill became the Minister of Education, and the church called the Rev. Kelly Sasser to be a full-time minister, dividing his time serving as a permanent youth minister and as a minister to children and their families. Previously, Duke Divinity School interns had served as youth minister, changing every year. With Sasser's arrival, a period of stability and growth began in the church's youth group.

And the process of converting the ladies' parlor into a chapel began with a generous donation from Earnest and Catherine Price. Worth Lutz made beautiful wood furniture for the chapel, and it was named the Catherine Elizabeth Price Chapel in honor of the Price's late daughter.

In March 2003, United States forces invaded Iraq. Iraq, as part of the settlement of the 1991 conflict, had agreed to let UN officials inspect and verify that they were not developing "weapons of mass destruction." The U.S., relying on bad intelligence, insisted that the Iraqis had such weapons and invaded.

The phrase "shock and awe" was introduced into the American vocabulary as citizens watched the massive bombing on their television screens. The church remained open for prayer. Williams preached a strong anti-war message, particularly this war. There was less opposition to his message than there had been in 1991. In January 2004, the Bush administration conceded that the weapons of mass destruction it was searching for did not exist. "We were almost all wrong," a chief weapons inspector testified to Congress. The next year, a presidential commission reached the same conclusion.

# # #

For many of these years of Williams's ministry, the church was considering its relationship with homosexual Christians. It was not alone. In 1988 a nationwide survey showed 11.6 percent of respondents thought gay people should have the right to marry. Thirty years later, 68 percent of Americans surveyed thought so. It is the most dramatic swing in public attitude ever charted by social scientists.

That one specific right—the right to marry—was part of a larger movement of general acceptance of and support for gay and lesbian people. Many things contributed, among them the activism triggered by the AIDS epidemic. Television shows, timidly at first, began to include gay characters. The "Don't Ask, Don't Tell" policy in the military which began under President Clinton in 1994, prohibited the military from taking action against closeted homosexuals while still allowing discrimination against anyone who was openly homosexual. At the time, it was viewed as a step forward; previously no gay people were allowed in the military, closeted or otherwise. By 2011, Don't Ask, Don't Tell had become an untenable remnant of anti-gay prejudice and was ended by President Obama and replaced with a non- discrimination policy. The next year, Obama announced his support of gay marriage, citing his personal evolution.

As the nation's views on homosexuality began to shift, some churches began studying and questioning the relationship between Christianity and homosexuality.

The issue took center stage in North Carolina Baptist circles in 1991 and 1992, when Pullen Memorial Baptist Church in Raleigh and Olin T. Binkley Baptist Church in Chapel Hill faced the issue of the role and rights of gay Christians in a public way.

Pullen had been conducting study groups on homosexuality starting in 1990. In November 1991, Pullen's senior pastor, the Rev. Mahan Siler, told Pullen's deacons that two young men—one who had been a member of Pullen for two and a half years and his partner, a Methodist who visited Pullen occasionally—had asked him "to officiate at the blessing of their same gender union." He said he had counseled with the couple for three sessions and was "satisfied that the motivation for their request as well as their commitment to God, the church and each other warrant a positive response. In spite of the complexity and controversial nature of their request, I feel led by my best understanding to serve as pastor at such a ceremony of blessing and commitment."

He went on to acknowledge that he did not operate independently. "I want you to share with me the responsibility of seeking the mind of Christ in this matter," he told them.

The deacons, after much discussion, supported Siler's decision. And again after much impassioned discussion, the congregation supported Siler.

Rev. Siler held the service of blessing and commitment for the two men on March 15, 1992.

Meanwhile, down the road in Chapel Hill, Binkley plunged into its own debate when an openly gay divinity student from Duke asked to be licensed to preach. When the congregation voted to issue the license, one-third of its deacon board resigned, and about 30 families left.

Both congregations were promptly expelled by Baptist organizations, including the SBC and the state convention. The Raleigh Baptist Association met at Cary First Baptist and voted 568 to 144 to oust Pullen after 109 years. Siler estimated that Pullen lost twenty percent of its membership.

At Watts Street, the congregation followed the situations at their sister churches closely. Williams had been pastor at Watts Street for almost four years by this time, and he had experience in facing this issue from his previous church, Oakhurst Baptist in Decatur, GA.

In the early 1980s at Oakhurst, the congregation's first openly gay member had wanted to teach children in Sunday School, generating pushback from some of the members. Williams gave a long- remembered sermon on having no "second-class members" at Oakhurst. Williams's personal feelings had long been that gay Christians were entitled to full participation in the work, fellowship, and rituals of the church.

He wanted to send a letter from Watts Street to our sister churches expressing support for the autonomy of the local church, but deacons and some in the congregation were concerned that a letter of support would imply that we supported the decisions they had made— something Watts Street was not ready to do in 1992.

Janet Moore drafted a letter to our sister churches, saying that we were "currently unprepared to speak with one voice" but that the many who signed this letter wanted to "express our support and send individual messages of compassion."

Deacons at Watts Street held a one-day retreat to discuss how the church should handle the issue. The Adult Education Committee decided on a study and released a statement of intent entitled: "Why do we study the issue of homosexuality at WSBC?

"The issue of homosexuality creates turmoil all around us. We watch as the Southern Baptist Convention 'excommunicates' our sister churches, Pullen and Binkley, for their stand on the issue. Some are asking why we must enter these troubled waters and risk polarizing our congregation by discussing this volatile issue." As "conscientious Christians," church members can no longer ignore this issue, which touches many of our members. The committee stressed that there was no agenda behind the study.

"We recognize that there are legitimate differences of opinion about homosexuality among Christians of goodwill, all of whom hold the Bible as their religious authority. We do not expect that any unanimous consensus will result from our study." The statement went on to lay great stress that the goal was to learn and discuss differences, not to let them divide the congregation. "We must respect the right to dissent within our church ... we want to affirm at the beginning of our study ... that disagreement with a church vote does not mean the dissenter leaves the church. Our Baptist principle of the autonomy of the local church should be extended to the autonomy of the individual conscience."

The summer forum, "Homosexuality: An Attempt to Achieve a Christian Understanding," was very well attended. Leaders were trained, and neighborhood meetings were held to discuss the subject further in small groups. Those meetings were also well-received.

Through the discussions, while the church arrived at no decisions, policy statements, or votes, an earlier history reports that the congregation settled into a new openness and sort of "Don't Ask, Don't Tell" kind of policy of its own. The congregation hoped its gay members felt welcomed. Several gay members held important roles in the church; some members hoped that there was no need to discuss it further. Gay members did not necessarily feel that way. The issue would come back around.

Binkley and Pullen both paid a heavy price for their public stands, both in membership and divisiveness. As the congregations moved on, they considered how they could have handled the discussion better. Rev. Siler recalled, 30 years later, "It was messy, and people got hurt, and we hurt people. It was a great process but not a perfect process."

Binkley's pastor, the Rev. Linda Jordan, left shortly after. A recent history of Binkley by Andrew Gardner stressed the sexism inherent in Binkley's process. Jordan was Binkley's second pastor. The Rev. Robert Seymour had led Binkley since its founding in 1958, and when he retired, he continued to attend Binkley, contrary to the standard practice of the former pastor leaving completely to allow the new pastor to form their own relationship with the congregation. Gardner cites multiple incidents where the congregation turned to the ever- present Seymour for leadership instead of their current pastor. It is hard to disentangle how much of that was turning to the man who had been your leader for thirty years and how much it was because Seymour was a man with a wife and family while Jordan was a single woman.

John Blevins, the divinity student who requested licensure, said he and Jordon were totally unprepared for the controversy his request unleashed. He went on to be a chaplain in Chicago, where his church said they would ordain him, but somehow never managed to set up the council to do it. From there, he went to Oakhurst Baptist Church (after Williams had left). In 1992, the ABCUSA adopted a theological statement that homosexuality was incompatible with Christian teaching. Several years later, the ABC ruled that all openly gay people would stay where they were in the ordination process, which meant Blevins would never be ordained. He gave up. He went on to a distinguished career at the intersection of public health and faith with the Rollins School of Public Health at Emory University and said he looks for opportunities to minister. He returned and spoke at Binkley in 2019.

After the licensing vote, Binkley committed itself to continuing the study of faith and sexuality and adopted an inclusive policy statement in 1994. In 1998, Binkley joined the Association of Welcoming and Affirming Baptists (AWAB). Pullen had been one of the churches to join AWAB when it was founded in 1993.

Several points emerged from both congregations on how to handle such potentially volatile discussions within a church family. They suggested talking about the general issue before there is a specific congregational situation to navigate and personalities are involved. Be sure and give the congregation time to consider and many, many opportunities to learn about the issue while accepting that those opposed will never have enough time or information. Openness on the part of deacons and church council on discussions going on is crucial. Pullen was fortunate to have a veteran pastor at the helm; Binkley said having a new pastor and one who was a woman made things more difficult as other issues got drawn into their debate. Their report quotes one lesbian member as saying that Binkley was not a safe place to have that discussion at that time. Listening in love and respecting disagreement is crucial and not always easy. Binkley's report summed it up: "Keep the faith and live in hope."

In 1999, the Alliance of Baptists issued a report from its Task Force on Human Sexuality and encouraged members to discuss it. The same year, the ABCUSA rejected several AWAB churches and reaffirmed a 1992 policy that said homosexuality is incompatible with Christian teaching. Next year, the Cooperative Baptist Fellowship adopted a policy against hiring gay people.

In January 2000, after paying close attention to lessons learned from Pullen and Binkley, Watts Street's church council created a task force to study the church's attitude towards homosexuality, chaired by Darryl Powell. Williams postponed his sabbatical leave to help lead the congregation through its discernment process. Great emphasis was placed on the process being open and transparent; some felt like Binkley had not been open with the congregation or with the press and had paid a high price for it.

Bob Helwig and Gordon Whitaker

Gordon Whitaker and Bob Helwig, a couple who would have a profound influence on Watts Street's actions moving ahead, joined the church after the Pullen and Binkley crisis. They joined separately, not advertising that they were a couple. Reading through the church's 75th history, Whitaker remembers encountering the account of the 1992 events and settling into the informal "don't ask, don't tell" way of dealing with homosexual Christians.

When I read the end of that sentence in their history, a shiver went through my body.... Did this mean that Bob and I might be asked to leave Watts Street church if certain members 'found out' we were a gay couple? That is what the U.S. Military policy states: you can be who you are unless the authorities find out. If they find out, you are kicked out.

As the church began its study two years later, Williams wrote, "The place of gay and lesbian people in American society is a pervasive, insistent issue that cannot be ignored." Watts Street had been welcoming without a statement, he said, citing the "gentle leadership" from Gordon Whitaker, Bob Helwig, Stuart Wells, and Leslie Webster—"people we know and love." The goal was to educate, share stories, and meet pastoral needs. "In this process, it is more important how we talk to one another than any end that might happen.

"As your pastor, I want to be clear, from my own experience and faith, that I believe in the open acceptance of all people, regardless of distinction. It is Jesus who invites all believers to the Communion Table, and we simply receive those who come.... Where we have disagreements, I hope we will speak them openly, in love, with respect. We don't always have to agree, but we must always seek to understand one another," Williams wrote.

The task force held small group meetings, encouraged gay members and their families to share their stories, and published a resource list and answers to frequently asked questions. They began working on a welcoming statement. "We want to draft a statement that captures the truth and spirit of what the Watts Street congregation believes about welcoming people to membership in our church." Several drafts were considered and discussed. To get an idea of where the congregation stood as a whole, the task force conducted a survey.

The survey, sometimes referred to as a vote in the minutes, aimed at a consensus. The concern was that asking for a yes or no vote on affirming gay members would prove too divisive. The survey asked for reactions to three options: a draft of a welcoming statement, a revised statement, and having no welcoming statement. Members were asked to rank each statement on a scale of 1 to 6, from strongly agree to strongly disagree. A final question asked if members at Watts Street supported ceremonies blessing same-sex couples.

Each of the three welcoming statements earned a majority of favorable votes. More than 120 members voted and between 64 percent and 76 percent approved of the specific statements. But a majority—almost 60 percent—reported that they would not like to see ceremonies in church blessing same-sex unions.

Many in the church expected the task force's work would lead to a vote. In the spring of 2001, a vote seemed imminent.

The survey results were tabulated and shared in March. In April,

Powell, writing for the task force, told the church council that task force members had been surprised by the intensity of the reaction they received. "While church members perceive themselves as accepting of homosexual Christians, there is considerable anxiety about how that acceptance should be shown." Those opposed "hold their views very strongly.... If some in the church do not want to express a welcome, then the church as a whole is not, in fact, welcoming."

The congregation did include some outspoken opponents of a welcoming statement. Billy Griffin was one of the most vocal, criticizing the process and saying adopting a welcoming statement would cost the congregation any relationships with Black churches and get Watts Street kicked out of the North Carolina Baptists. Phil Pearce expressed concerns that the task force had been selected to adopt a welcoming statement—not to consider the issue from all points of view.

At the church meeting on May 20, 2001, with the ad hoc committee and the church council recommending that no vote be taken for fear of dividing the church, the congregation voted to not vote on adopting a welcoming and affirming statement "at this time."

But while voting would have come with consequences, so did not voting. Many members were disappointed, including Williams. The fact that leaders in the church considered the congregation too divided to hold a vote was a bitter pill.

In the Baptist church where Williams grew up in Aberdeen, North Carolina, the members held a vote on whether to seat Negroes on the floor of the church or on the balcony. The church voted to not seat them at all. The pastor, Denny Spear, resigned in protest. His action left a strong impression, and Williams considered whether this was a moment he needed to do the same. He reached out to Mahan Siler, his friend and the senior pastor during Pullen's struggles with the issue, who told him few churches had gotten so far with the issue and to hang in there.

Whitaker, a member of the task force, struggled with his own disappointment. In choosing to stay with the congregation he had come to love, he wrote that the process had taught him a lot about love. "I thank God for leading me to Watts Street and bringing us through this last year's experiences so that we could draw closer together and love more freely." A vote itself does not make a church welcoming. "We either welcome all people or we don't Sometimes, however, the discipline of loving the community and wanting to preserve it may be more important than the exercise of our individuality—our own understanding of what is right and good. I think that, for me, this is such a time. I have learned that I love my brothers and sisters at Watts Street, even when they exasperate me, even when they hurt me, even when I see them hurting others. I believe that my call is to try to reach out to them, just as it is my call to try to reach out to those whom they reject. I have learned that it is hard to do that."

And although there was no welcoming statement, changes occurred. A group calling themselves Out and About, consisting of some gay members and those who supported them, began meeting for a potluck supper and conversation every month.

Chris and Jim Arges in the Gay Pride Parade.

And Darryl Powell, Bill McCraw, and Ken Ellis decided to make a movie for the church. They titled it "Just as I am," and they interviewed Watts Street members—gay members and families of gay individuals, talking about how the issue of homosexuality had affected them personally. The sense that homosexuality was an issue that did not affect the Watts Street congregation crumbled.

Outside of Watts Street, the battlelines became ever more clearly drawn. In 2004, in response to the North Carolina Baptists "disfellowshipping" churches for their acceptance of gay members, Watts Street considered leaving. The May church night included much discussion, with members considering whether to go ahead and leave or wait to be kicked out. Some still hoped that some sort of compromise could be worked out. The major concern among many was whether the church could still have access to Fort Caswell, the site of so many wonderful memories for Watts Street. The church could still use the facility, for a slightly higher fee.

The congregation voted to leave.

In 2007, the church took up the issue again when the church council created an ad hoc committee to "provide guidance toward a church decision on a welcoming statement, its use, that may include membership in AWAB (Association of Welcoming and Affirming Baptists), the authorization of ordination to ministry and the blessing of unions without regard to sexual orientation." On January 1, 2008, a new statement appeared in the bulletin, saying it was the practice of Watts Street to "welcome and affirm all person, regardless of race, class, origin, sexual orientation, or any other distinction." The group was careful to say practice—not policy.

That spring, Helwig and Whitaker had a covenant ceremony, which they shared with the church at large. On May 24, they stood at the front of the church and heard Williams preach a homily on love casting out fear. The two men had already been partners for 37 years, and "for us as a church, this is our opportunity to offer the blessing of this faith community. That means this is a great day, a holy day, a historic day, a day when, as Isaiah states, 'God is doing a new thing.' (Isaiah 43:19.)" Williams urged those gathered to say no to loveless fear and yes to fearless love.

It was a high point in the life of the congregation. The church published a booklet of reactions to the ceremony. Diane Eubanks

Hill, who said Helwig and Whitaker were the first openly gay couple she knew, wrote about their "patient ministry ... daring to become more and more transparent with each passing year." Darryl Powell wrote about the church's unwillingness to take a stand earlier. Powell said Whitaker and Helwig "simply changed the culture, just by being themselves—an old married couple."

In 2009, the church took up the issue of joining AWAB, and despite the joy and fellowship created by the covenant ceremony, it was still controversial for some. The ground was carefully prepared, with discussions and the opportunity to ask questions. Williams preached on it that morning and began the meeting with a recap of the church's experiences with this issue. He stressed that this was a place for genuine humility. He urged people to vote their consciences and leave friends. Jim Drennan, who had led the committee, made the motion for the welcoming statement and to join AWAB. Phil Pearce made a substitute motion that we adopt the welcoming statement without joining AWAB. It is a sign of how far the congregation had come that those opposed to joining AWAB supported a formal welcoming statement. Another proposal was for a statement that acknowledged the diversity of opinion in the congregation. At times, the meeting grew heated. When a long-time member expressed concern over the $1,200 AWAB membership fee, others clamored that they would pay it. He wryly expressed his hope that they would remember that when the bill came due. His family had given generously to the church since its founding. Those at the meeting paused in their discussion long enough to stand and applaud him and his families many gifts to the church.

After three hours, the vote was taken and the motion passed 112 to 16. Clay Chandler then made a personal statement about working with people on both sides of the issue and asked everyone to respect and contact those who felt so badly hurt.

The next Sunday's bulletin contained the new welcoming statement: It is the practice and policy of Watts Street Baptist Church to welcome and affirm all persons, regardless of race, class, origin, sexual orientation, or any other distinction.

The relationship with the Yates Baptist Association did not survive this move. Church members reported that contacts with Yates convinced them that Yates wanted Watts Street gone, and it would be easier all around if we left rather than force the issue.

Watts Street left.

In 2011, WSBC was part of a press conference held on its front steps to announce the church's support of a lawsuit against proposed Amendment One, which went on to pass in North Carolina. Amendment One, which made same-sex marriages illegal and forbade clergy to perform them, was approved in a state-wide referendum in 2012 and declared unconstitutional and overturned by a North Carolina judge in 2014. The next year, the U.S. Supreme Court ruled that same-sex marriage was a right.

As homosexuality gained more mainstream acceptance, other issues came to the fore. Watts Street, its congregation, including several transgender youth, held a workshop in 2014 to learn more about gender identity, gender expression, and other issues, trying to apply the gospel message of love and acceptance to all.

# # #

Williams retired in February 2012 after almost 24 years at Watts Street. Two years later, he was named Pastor Emeritus, the first such Watts Street has had. He left with an appreciation of a balanced life, something he had learned while at Watts Street.

Williams recalled that he plunged into his work at church. "I wanted to be a good pastor; I also wanted to be involved in the community," he said. He wound up in the hospital twice—in 1989 and 1993 for problems exacerbated by stress. "My system couldn't take it."

He left for his first sabbatical at a monastery in 1995 drained. He gradually learned balance, that social justice and community work cannot be maintained long term without spiritual practice. The practice can be prayer, sitting in silence, yoga, meditation, mindfulness, walking in the woods—whatever brings one into the spiritual presence. "Unless you can nurture that, you won't last," Williams said. "You cannot pour out of a pitcher what is not in it."

He has been meeting with a spiritual practice group, Peace Hill, since 1995. Avila, a retreat in northern Durham County, is now home to Peace Hill. Its mission is "to nurture and teach contemplative and restorative practices to build a more compassionate and just society." This work is vital "to the good work of individuals and organizations to create a better and more sustainable world."

Williams also began working with a group called End Poverty in Durham. While he left the pulpit behind, his passion for missions is as strong as ever.

Members of the Peace and Reconciliation group and other Watts Street members showed up to take part in the Moral Monday protests at the state legislature in Raleigh in 2013.

God is always telling a bigger story than we are.

--The Rev. Dorisanne Cooper

The Dorisanne Cooper Years, 2014 to present

After two years of soul-searching and hard work, Watts Street called the Reverend Dorisanne Cooper of Lake Shore Baptist Church in Waco, Texas, to be the next pastor. She arrived in Durham in July 2014 with her husband, David Tatum, and their son Adam.

The Cooper-Tatum family, the Reverend Dorisanne Cooper, David and Adam Tatum

Cooper had grown up in Waco. Both her parents were professors at Baylor University, and she attended Baylor for college. Next came Princeton Theological Seminary in New Jersey. It is a Presbyterian seminary, and as Cooper says, "It opened up my eyes to what women can do in the church."

"There were so many women there that were planning to be pastors and I had never experienced that as something people would readily accept," Cooper said, saying she had heard of one Baptist woman senior pastor before divinity school. "I'd not experienced a woman saying, 'I want to be a pastor' in Baptist life and the whole room not going quiet in response."

She began seminary not knowing if she wanted to spend her professional life in the institutional church, but knowing the study and time spent there would become part of whatever profession she chose. After her first year at Princeton, she served as a summer intern at College Park Baptist Church in Greensboro, North Carolina, working for her former youth pastor, Michael Usey. After graduation, she returned to the church in Greensboro and stayed for six years.

College Park was a place where the general attitude was, "Honestly, we're not sure we believe in the institutional church either, but come on over and let's try it out together," Cooper recalled. "It was a wonderful place and where I was ordained." She also finds similarities with Watts Street and Lake Shore. "They are places where people don't have blinders on about what church is— it's people and all the delight and flaws we bring to the world."

As for the choice about entering into life in the institutional church, "Ultimately, for me, the point was, I need to live faith in community, not just as an individual. I need people prodding and challenging and providing support for one another as they try and live out their faith. Those were the best things that led me into the church and finding churches that said, 'Yes, there's a place for you.'"

After serving as associate pastor for five years, she served as the senior pastor for six months in College Park while Usey was on a sabbatical and learned that the role suited her. "I honestly didn't realize it before that time," she recalled. "I thought, 'I see now this is where I fit. It could work.'"

Along the way, Dorisanne developed what she says as she baptizes people. The traditional words have been, "I baptized you, my brother (or sister), in the name of the Father, the Son, and the Holy Spirit." She says that, and then continues: "One God, mother of us all."

"It is just what I have always done. It connects us to the great commandment, and also reflects our ever-expanding notion of God."

From College Park, she was called as pastor of Lake Shore Baptist Church, returning to her hometown of Waco for 12 years. "It was wonderful. I loved being a part of a college town church. About half of our church members were connected to Baylor in some way, and I loved the thoughtful, committed ways they approached their faith."

Lake Shore's building includes an all-purpose hall that serves as a sanctuary, fellowship hall, and most other things. A kitchen stands at one end, and a pulpit, baptistry, and choir loft at the other. Though they had initially planned to, the congregation ultimately chose not to build a separate sanctuary but continue to use the same space as the sanctuary on Sunday mornings and the fellowship hall during the week.

At the time, Lake Shore was the only Baptist church in Waco affiliated with the Alliance of Baptists, a progressive church in a generally conservative town. Cooper was on the board of Planned Parenthood, the church sponsored an educational event with them every year, and the CEO was a member of her congregation. Thus, the church was the scene of regular protest. One year, a local group set up protests at what they named "the ten gates of Hell" and listed Lake Shore as one of them. In an interview in the Waco Tribune-Herald, one of the protestors said it was because Cooper preached a gospel of "unbridled lust and sex without consequences." It was a comment that bothered her until a church member kidded her and asked if they could print it on a T-shirt.

"That congregation taught me so much because I was honestly

pretty scared by all of this, and I didn't know how to respond," she said. After the T-shirt comment, she realized the church could approach the whole thing with some humor and simply accept that others did not understand who they were.

# # #

Watts Street had been on a two-year odyssey to find Cooper. Williams had been the pastor for 24 years, and for many members of the church, he was the only pastor they had known at Watts Street. They needed time to grieve, to think, and to plan. The church turned to the Center for Congregational Health in Winston-Salem, a non-denominational organization that aims to help provide leadership for churches in transition or crisis. The Rev. Gene Derryberry served as an interim pastor at Watts Street from May 2012 to May 2013, helping with meetings where the congregation worked hard to consider what they wanted for the future of their community. A 14-member transition team was created to guide the church through a process of self- examination to clarify who it was and what the church should look for in a new pastor. The team deliberately moved relatively slowly, following advice from experts in congregational transitions. As a guideline, the experts suggested that for each year a previous pastor served, the transition should take about one month. Coincidentally, this transition lasted just over 24 months. The transition team generated a profile of the church and a pastor profile. After a year of work, it recommended that the church create a pastor search committee. For the second year of the transition, the congregation made the decision to have lay leadership, and the church staff led the church until a pastor was chosen.

The search committee collected names and recommendations and shared the profile of the church widely, asking if those recommended would like to be considered. Cooper, who frequently got letters from churches who wanted to consider a woman pastor who had experience, said she answered the letter from Watts Street just before the deadline. The profile looked very appealing.

The committee received materials from 100 pastors. They selected 20 and asked them to send copies of sermons. They reviewed the sermons and selected six people to interview.

Cooper said she drove two hours from Waco to Austin, Texas, to be interviewed remotely at the setup at Cisco, the employer of one committee member. Being interviewed remotely would become common following the COVID epidemic, but in 2013 it was high-tech. Cooper said she was very impressed with the committee, all arrayed on a wall of screens across from here. "All I could think of was wondering whether I was just one giant head on their screen," she laughed.

Following that interview, she visited Durham twice to meet with them in person. "Ultimately, I just fell in love with the whole committee. I wanted to do church with these people." She met with church leaders and staff as well. On the second visit, she preached, and the congregation formally called her.

Cooper knew she was coming in after Mel Williams, a dynamic leader. "My leadership style is one where I'm going to come in and listen and help discern and see what you are thinking and how to get there together. It works well for me but can be uncomfortable for some. Sometimes they think that's not really leadership—that leadership has to involve telling people where we're supposed to go, what we're supposed to do, but that wasn't going to be my style."

Her leadership style is reflected in her preaching. She invites the congregation to consider the text with her—"My stance is not 'I have this to say about the text to you sitting across from me.' It's more like, 'Come around to my side of the table or let me come sit with you and let's look at this together.'" So she and the congregation are studying together in a sense. She strives to "balance in my preaching highlighting injustices and our call to address them and pastoral care for people who are aching from the state of the world." In doing that, she also brings a disciplined approach to preaching from Biblical texts and the Lectionary.

She felt drawn to Watts Street because it was already doing the work. "There wasn't confusion about who we are as a church. It was well established that this was a very social justice-oriented church, that we were going to be engaged in the world and concerned about the world and all the things that faith means to me."

The challenge is to keep doing it and figure out how to sustain one's spirit as you do. "We want to change the world, but it turns out that's really hard to do and there are going to be a lot more failures than success when it comes to justice. So how do we sustain ourselves for the long term? What practices do we put into place to nurture our spirits and stay about this work day in and out?" It's a balance of looking inward as well as outward, so you can be about the work year after year.

# # #

Cooper was one year into working on these goals at Watts Street when she was diagnosed with breast cancer just before Thanksgiving in 2015. It was a shock, and each time she met with her doctors, it seemed that things got more serious. Eventually, she would require surgery, chemotherapy, and radiation.

The chemo bothered her the most. It meant losing her hair, and she was concerned about looking sick in front of the congregation. "I didn't know a pastor who had been sick and kept on pastoring. I didn't have a model for that," she said. "I didn't know how to talk to the church about it." She said one pastor advised her not to tell the congregation anything until she knew exactly what would be involved with her treatment and prognosis, but Cooper found that did not work for her. "I could not do it. I could not preach about Advent and waiting that year and not share that I was waiting on something very personal. And didn't know what was going to happen." So she wrote the church a letter, explaining the situation and asking them to wait with her.

"People were really kind. People here have been through life," she recalled. She and Adam (then 9 years old) met with children's Sunday School classes before her treatments began so they could ask questions and understand that she would lose her hair and have to take certain precautions to stay healthy. They ended up writing her letters to keep her apprised of their lives in the meantime. She kept an online journal shared with the congregation to communicate throughout her treatments while she couldn't greet before or after worship services. While she was having chemotherapy, they arranged for another preacher for every three weeks, timing it so that the week that the treatment hit her the hardest, she did not have to preach. The Personnel Committee encouraged her to work when she was able; and to rest when she was not. And then after a year of treatment, they encouraged her to go ahead and take a vacation with her family. Cooper was exhausted and deeply appreciative of a little extra time to recover. In one memorable episode, in the middle of her chemo, she was able to attend the All-Ages Beach Retreat, fresh with a bright green wig. She was greeted at the retreat by a memory book full of notes, poems, pictures, and other items prepared from individual expressions of love from members of the congregation. She related that she felt a surge of energy at the retreat, even as fatigue was a constant part of her experience at that stage of chemo.

"I will never forget their generosity throughout that entire year," she said.

#

In the larger Baptist world during these years, things were shifting. When the church left the Yates Baptist Association and the ABCUSA, and the CBF expressed less than full support for gay Christians, the church decided to increase their contributions to the Alliance of Baptists and decrease it to the ABC and CBF.

In 2018, it was time to revisit the issue. "We will explore both what it might mean to 'leave' some of our denominations and different options for what it might mean to continue a relationship with ABCUSA and CBF, but with intentional engagement toward full acceptance (e.g., designated giving, specific ways we will participate and advocate for change.)" The church invited in a consultant, met in small groups, and discovered that the issue was still very painful for many. Although a substantial portion of the congregation came from other faith traditions, there were many who still struggled with reconciling their current beliefs and their SBC heritage. There were strongly held beliefs, with some that Watts Street should remain in these groups and try and affect change, and with others that the only way truly to show solidarity with the LGBTQ members was not to sit at tables where they weren't fully welcome. Cooper led a months-long discernment process that allowed voices to be heard but did not result in a consensus recommendation. A small group working with Cooper to guide the process produced a "stay and fight" set of recommendations, but that did not resolve the issue.

Like most difficult congregational decisions, this one took time. As the recommendations began to be implemented, mostly through budget adjustments, those who were not in the "stay and fight" camp continued to push for the church to leave organizations that discriminated. That effort led the church to ask the Denominational Relations Committee to revisit the recommendations.

Two years later, in 2020, the Denominational Relations committee came to the decision that the pain of those who were not fully included needed to be the deciding factor for the congregation and made three recommendations, and the congregation approved them by a vote of 85 to 5, with 4 abstentions. The congregation ended up encouraging individuals to maintain their work as individuals with the CBF but decided that they would no longer financially support them as a group. The church's ABC affiliation was transferred from the American Baptist Churches of the South to the American Baptist Churches of the Rochester Genesee region, where other open and affirming churches had found refuge as well. This process was, in Watts Street's tradition, too slow for many. But with Cooper's patient and gentle leadership, it resulted in a decision that had staying power and was accepted by all sides.

During these years, the Creation Care ministry was revitalized, and the church made serious efforts toward sustainability. A textile recycling bin was placed in the parking lot, and the church began composting in a major way. The composting was so effective that the dumpster was replaced by two roadside trash bins. Plans were made to include solar panels in the church's future renovations.

In 2017, when neighboring Beth El synagogue needed to move their preschool out of its building to treat mold, they moved into Watts Street and are still there at this writing. The congregation made a commitment to paying a living wage, something it was already striving to do.

In another major issue addressed during this period, the staff was restructured after long-time minister the Rev. Diane Eubanks Hill retired. The Church Council named a task force to examine various staff models and research the best path forward for the congregation. Ultimately, due largely to budget pressures, Hill's position as Minister to Adults was not filled, and the church decided to continue with three pastors instead of four. The Rev. Esther Soud Parker, who had been hired as the minister to Children and their Families in 2013, added Congregational Care to her responsibilities, including many of the responsibilities of Christian Education. And the Rev. Kelly Sasser, Minister to Youth and their Families, added Community Life to his responsibilities, taking on the leadership of the church's Mission efforts. Sherrill Figuera joined the staff in 2016 as the new office manager when Mary Hermanson retired after many years. Figuera took on an increased role in building management, bringing several years of experience with her.

Children form a chain to emphasize how we are linked together.

The church continued its work with the Walltown neighborhood and like much of the country as instances of police violence against Black people became daily fare on the evening news, considered anew the racist nature of country and the history of racism in the church writ large.

Vacation Bible School

Then came COVID.

# # #

A cluster of patients in China's Hubei Province experienced a mysterious illness in December of 2019. It was the first sign of a pandemic that would kill millions of people worldwide and radically transform life for several years.

It took less than three months to spread to the United States. Borders were closed, gatherings were canceled, and Americans were told to stay at home. Hospitals were flooded with infected patients, and New York City turned to refrigerated trucks to serve as impromptu morgues. People were terrified and bewildered.

It hit North Carolina on a lovely spring day as many were following one of the state's favorite rituals, the ACC men's basketball tournament in Greensboro. The games were being played without a crowd in an attempt to reduce the spread of COVID. On

March 11, day two for the ACC, Congress heard testimony from Anthony Fauci that things were about to get much worse with the epidemic. Fauci would become a household name over the next two years with his daily briefings on COVID. As he testified on March 11, the World Health Organization declared COVID a pandemic. That night, President Donald Trump addressed the nation, announcing plans to close the borders.

Still, the next morning, Florida State and Clemson players took the court to warm up for the game. But just before the game was to begin, ACC officials announced that the tournament was canceled. They handed the trophy to Florida State as the number one seed and sat back to await developments.

Developments came quickly as all college and professional sports canceled their seasons, and schools and businesses closed. Public spaces were deserted.

Over the next two and a half years, 1.1 million Americans would die of COVID, 29,000 of them in North Carolina and 397 of them in Durham. The WHO estimates almost seven million people died worldwide—a number that is assuredly a serious undercount.

America's churches responded in different ways, with the leadership of mainline denominations and various other faiths urging some kind of COVID precautions. Even so, the response of churches was widely varied. Some congregations vowed that God would keep them safe and continued to meet; others shut down completely.

At Watts Street, trying to be safe and be a church, it was a time of constant shifting, doing the best they could with the information they had. In the weeks before the national shutdown, the decisions were about things like whether the staff should serve Wednesday night supper instead of having people serve themselves to minimize contact. And passing the offering plate seemed like something that maybe should stop for a while. Then came the realization that there should be no Wednesday night suppers to serve or worship services in which to pass the plate.

Cooper said she remembers vividly, the morning after the ACC cancelation, consulting with Mitch Heflin, a doctor and a church member, about what the church should do. In 48 hours, the advice had changed from being careful to a full shutdown.

"It happened fast," Cooper said. "At first, we hoped by Easter we would come back. Remember 'Flatten the curve'?" Flattening the curve was one of the initial hopes, the idea that if everyone stayed home for a few weeks, we could slow the spread of COVID to a more manageable level, and there would be no spike in cases. "There was always something changing. It took a while to realize how long it was going to last."

Watts Street went online with a service on the first Sunday, March 15. "We livestreamed the service to our Facebook page from the sanctuary. It was very much a bubblegum and shoestring setup," Cooper recalled. The church's three ministers—Cooper, Sasser, Parker—Director of Music Ministries Melody Zentner and organist Tom Bloom streamed from a church laptop they suddenly realized was old. In the weeks following, they divided up duties that needed to be covered, with Sasser taking over the new technology responsibilities.

What church looked like during COVID

The church had taken steps to improve its technological capabilities before COVID hit. Figuera said that by late 2019, the staff had all their documents on a shared drive accessible from their laptops at church or home. "It was almost like something was preparing us for this." (Cooper insists the 'something' was Figuera.)

Just weeks before the shutdown, the Information Technology Committee held its first Zoom meeting. "We had just gotten a Zoom account, but most of us didn't know how to use it," Cooper recalled. In fact, the reaction to the first Zoom meeting was one of wonder— "You are never going to believe this—they had a meeting on video from their houses! We are so advanced! This is some high-tech stuff!" As COVID hit, of course, that then became the norm.

The staff soon learned that live streaming offered a chance for too many things to go wrong with the equipment they had and they began recording portions of the service. They would each record from home, Bloom recorded from the sanctuary, post to the cloud, and Sasser would take it off the cloud and produce a worship service. Doing it this way allowed church members to participate by making recordings as well. "There was some nice creativity to that. It allowed for a better experience of being able to see folks besides just the staff guiding worship each week," Cooper recalled.

At first, Sasser would record Zentner singing the hymns in the sanctuary. That changed when he started adding in hymns Watts Street had recorded as part of its weekly services over the years. Members would read scriptures from their homes, and it would be incorporated into the service. The congregation was encouraged to attend online and enact all the parts of the service they could at home. The staff packed worship bags for special services—a candle, a bun, and a package of hot chocolate mix for the Christmas love feast and ashes for Ash Wednesday. Parker recalled getting little plastic condiment containers and filling them with ashes to hand out. The staff got creative in their efforts to keep the rhythm of the church year and to keep the congregation connected. The annual church bazaar was held outdoors, using an online ordering system.

Before COVID was over, the church would dramatically increase its technological equipment and abilities, and Zoom meetings would become standard.

Church meetings during COVID

The amount of decision-making required to meet the changing situation could be overwhelming. Cooper said, "Pivot, pivot, pivot" became the motto. The staff pulled together an advisory board, aiming for a good cross-section of the congregation, to help make decisions with them. And each decision felt loaded with more questions. "Every decision created questions. When we decided to worship outdoors, we then had to ask, but can people go inside if they need to? Can people go into the bathrooms? Should we go in one by one? There was so much we didn't know," Cooper recalled.

Throughout the lockdown, Cooper was part of a weekly online meeting with city and health department officials for Durham clergy to pass on the most recent information. "It was a really helpful thing the city put together," she said. "It helped us make connections with those not just across faiths and denominations, but across racial and economic lines as well."

One of the decisions the church had to make was whether to accept Payroll Protection Plan funding from the government, offered to help organizations cover their payroll in the uncertain days of not knowing what the financial impact of the shutdown would be. The

Church Council and the staff were a bit conflicted about what the consequences might be and whether there were church/state conflict risks. Ultimately, they did decide to accept the money ($62,000) with the understanding that if there were a chance in the future to pay an equitable amount forward, they would come back to the conversation. As it turned out, at the end of 2021, even though the pandemic was still in force, the church finished the year with sufficient revenues from congregational contributions to cover expenses, so the church elected to use the surplus generated by contributions plus the PPP loan to support Black-led or Black-owned non-profits who may have felt the economic and social impact of COVID in a more intense way.

Interestingly, in a series of coincidences, the church had two unexpected capital expenses. First, the need for streaming services required better equipment, but rather than use the surplus, two church members donated funds to purchase the needed equipment— the church's commitment to work in the community trumped its own self- interest. Then, at about the same time that the decisions were made to support the black-led nonprofits, a major electrical failure in the church's wiring necessitated a major repair. The cost? $62,000, almost exactly the PPP loan. Fortunately, the church's building fund reserves were adequate to cover this repair. Thus, while there were two possible uses for the surplus to benefit "us," the church enthusiastically supported the "Missions" use of the funds. "It was a Spirit-filled conversation and decision," Cooper said, speaking of Church Council's move to give the entire amount away.

From the beginning of the pandemic, the staff set their priorities. Sasser said they thought about what was important to the church: "our connection to God and to each other." So, the worship service remained a priority, a group Cooper had started in 2016, For the Living of These Days, continued to meet online every Wednesday evening, and many Sunday School classes met weekly online.

And the church decided to be cautious in its health decisions. Early in the pandemic in Durham, a child had died. Her death and the concerns of older members and those with young children helped shape the response. "We are going to function in practice for the most vulnerable among us. We said that from the beginning,"

Cooper said. "We masked until everyone was eligible for the vaccine. We felt comfortable erring on the side of caution."

"I'm sure there were people who were frustrated or even irritated that we wore masks for as long as we did, but they really didn't complain," Cooper said. People understood that they were wearing masks at church for their community. "We had a community that got it," Sasser said. "That was a gift." "Love your neighbor and mask on" became a church motto.

Figuring out how the youth group was going to function in a pandemic took a little time. At first, youth group meetings on Zoom were "close to tortuous," Sasser said. Kids were hurting, struggling with online school, and missing major events. In an attempt to make up for the loss of a senior prom, Sasser held a prom online. Things like that worked for the spring of 2020. In June, he launched the second phase; they would meet outside, masked and in small groups. He grouped the youth into pods to reduce exposure and met every Tuesday and Thursday with one pod, alternating service projects and social time, so each youth had something to attend once every two weeks. "One of the cool things about that was I got to spend a lot of concentrated time with all these pod groups, and that was very enjoyable," Sasser said. "For the kids, there was nothing else going on. And they were available. And they came to these things. And it was great!"

In February 2022, almost exactly two years into the shutdown, the youth group took an overnight retreat. They masked, ate outside, and even drove with the windows open. "The mentality was, we've got to keep going. We're going to find ways to get together," Sasser said.

At his end-of-the-year program and slide show in 2023, Sasser said the pictures of the seniors' time in youth group hit hard. Suddenly, everyone in the photos was in masks and physically apart. "Obviously, you do it in that situation because you love each other, and that's what love does, but it makes your heartache."

For Parker, working with younger children, Zoom was also a challenge. She taught Sunday School online for children and hosted a midweek program for preschoolers. She learned to keep things short. She even tried to do PASSPORTkids, a camp for children in the summer. "It was just awful," she laughed. She had good support from her parents, but keeping the children's attention was difficult. "I really gave it a good try."

The choir also felt the effects of COVID deeply. Singing was particularly risky in transmitting COVID, and the choir was not able to rehearse or lead in worship during the months of the shutdown. Zentner and Bloom arranged several outdoor rehearsals with folks spread out around the parking lot just to allow them to sing together.

The church missed two years of the All Ages Beach Retreat at Caswell and two years of Christmas Love Feasts in the sanctuary. When someone died, their loved ones were denied the comfort of bereavement rituals—the chance to gather and tell stories, the service itself, and the reception with hugs and tears. At first, families postponed funerals, hoping COVID would be over. Others chose to have Cooper conduct graveside services only. Weddings and child dedications were delayed. The isolation was overwhelming for many as the months rolled by with no end in sight.

Vaccines against COVID started to become available in December 2020. A massive vaccination campaign geared up, and on September 19, 2021, the church began holding its worship service outdoors and masked in the parking lot. The church held its first service in the sanctuary on November 28, 2021, the first Sunday in Advent. It was tempting to believe the end was in sight. But by Christmas, the Omicron variant had arrived and quickly spiked to high levels. The Christmas Eve service was held outdoors, and on December 26, the church returned to online completely.

And the world's other problems did not disappear because of COVID. America continued its racial reckoning as George Floyd died at the hands of police in Minneapolis on May 25, 2020. Video of a police officer kneeling on Floyd's neck for more than eight minutes inflamed the nation. On June 8, members of Watts Street and others joined in the protest, sitting in their cars or standing in the parking lot while the church bells rang for the length of time Floyd was pinned.

The church issued a call for a new mission group on Martin

Luther King Jr. Sunday in January 2021 to continue its work on racial reckoning. The group outlined a three-year plan of study and action. A program called 50 + 500 invited church members to work during the 50 days of the Pentecost season to take action against racism. Suggested actions included community service, study, advocacy, missions, reflection, or other activities that focused on dealing with racism. Individuals and groups well exceeded the goal, and it seeded a re-investment and deeper engagement in racial justice work for many in the congregation.

On March 6, 2022, the church again returned to meeting in person inside. Crowds did not rush back. Some members were still leery. Others had gotten out of the habit. Parker said the group hardest hit was the families with young children. The children were back in school or daycare, and the parents were back at work, but the family did not want to risk any further exposure. Many preschoolers were left with no working memory of church.

A continuity of leadership in some areas was also lost in the pandemic, Cooper said. Usually, the chair of a committee informally trains their successor as they move from year to year, but several committees have not met. The Bereavement Ministry had to begin again—for two years, there were no funeral receptions. Greeters and Ushers had aged out. People who had carried out church responsibilities season after season were done. The fellowship of Wednesday night—the sharing of joys and sorrows when all ages are gathered—was lost for two years. It took time and effort from the staff and a core group of leaders to rebuild some of the foundations that needed to be in place for a healthy, functioning congregation.

During their recording of worship, while there were clear benefits, Cooper learned she was not cut out for preaching online long-term. Preaching to a camera was a challenge that seemed just about getting comfortable with the mechanics at first, but ultimately still included an empty room. "For me, there is an energy on Sunday mornings in person that can't be manufactured. Preaching is a conversation to me and not being able to see people's eyes, faces, body language, even who is distracted or nodding off, really took its toll on my spirit in a deep way. I know we did what had to be done, but corporate worship includes being together. It includes the chatter before the service about what's going on in each other's lives. It includes watching children grow and change over time. It includes responses to music or, silence or prayers. Not having those things for a stretch was a lot more painful than I allowed myself to feel in the moment. Let's just say I won't be exploring televangelism anytime soon."

But there were gains, too, on balance. The lockdown showed many of us what it was to be homebound, Sasser pointed out. People who struggle with hearing reported that they could hear better online. Church became accessible in a new way, and people who had moved away or were unable to attend did not have to be cut off. People looking for a church could find us online. As our technology improved, Sasser said, we began to realize that this would be ongoing, it "pushed us into where we needed to be."

And the staff agreed there was resilience and a perspective gained. The community, with all the loss of physical time together, stayed connected and supported each other. Not everyone, but many stayed connected. "I have faith in this community, having gone through what we have gone through now," Figuera said.

The trend lines of mainline protestant churches have been pretty bleak for years, but "church is here, we are still here," Sasser said. Here, we focus on what is important—worship, community, and service.

The church learned, "We can go through pauses of things. We don't have to do every single thing all the time in the way we have always done it," Cooper said. "We can change some things and even find new life."

Gradually, more and more people returned. Through the pandemic, church finances remained stable, bucking a trend that hit many mainline congregations. A number of families that had moved to Durham during the pandemic were ready to find a church community and brought their energy and gifts into the mix. "There is a good energy to the church. These days of gathering and being together are a gift. We know that now, perhaps better than we ever have," Cooper says. Moving forward, the ability to attend church and hold committee meetings online will continue, allowing more people to participate.

# # #

As Watts Street continues to move an uncertain world, Cooper said the congregation aims to be a place motivated to continue living God's radical love in the world. "I've really been taken with a Walter Brueggemann quote in these days. He says, 'The prophetic tasks of the church are to tell the truth in a society that lives in illusion, grieve in a society that practices denial, and express hope in a society that lives in despair.'

"We know that living God's radical love doesn't mean a smooth path of delight in each moment. It means truth-telling, grieving, and hoping. I would add it means cultivating wonder and awe and rest as well.

"There is no question that huge strides for justice have been made inside and outside of the church since 1923, but there's still so much work to do," she said. "God's love is always telling a bigger story than we are. That's our reminder to ourselves and also to those who continue to cause so much harm in these days with fear and discrimination. The list is long of things that surely must grieve God: white supremacy, ongoing LGBTQ discrimination, Christian nationalism, and the ways fear has taken a deep hold in so many political decisions of our day.

"Add that and so much more to the ways that the life-giving ways of God are needed in the world. Let's just say the church is not going to run out of ways to be called any time soon, and so we'll keep heeding God's call to confession, renewal, and engagement as we move into the days, weeks, and years to come," she said.

Challenges for the church unique at this time include becoming a hybrid community, online and in person. And caring for the building, now a century old. "It's time to pay attention to our building and realize that it's a resource for us and can be for the community in ways we haven't explored," Cooper said. "It is going to take some attention. In all of it, I pray we'll stay open and curious about the future rather than anxious so that as a church, we become more deeply who we are meant to be."

Of the making of many books, there is no end.

Ecclesiastes 12:12

A Note on Sources and Other Things

I have drawn heavily on the church archives for this book, including the deacon minutes, the records of church meetings, church reports and plans, oral histories conducted by and with WSBC members, and other documents tucked away over the years. There are many treasures in the archives, and alas! many gaps.

The Durham newspapers have been a rich source, as have external oral history interviews– one by Baylor and one by Duke— with Warren Carr. C.S. Greene's lively autobiography (available in full at the Special Collections & Archives at Z. Smith Reynolds Library at Wake Forest University) is a treasure. The story about Warren Carr throwing a punch and having a black eye when the Princeton church called him came from Preaching and Professing: Sermons by a Teacher Seeking to Proclaim the Gospel, by Ralph C. Wood from Carr's Eulogy that Wood preached in 2007.

Several things that have passed into church legend have proved impossible to pin down. The story of the writing on the church doors in response to the church's stance on race exists only in Carr's interviews and in member's retellings over the years. There is no contemporaneous account, no newspaper mention. The degree to which services at Watts Street were racially integrated in the 1950s and 1960s is unrecoverable. We do know that no Black people joined the church during that time; we also know that some Black people attended services at least some time. The dates of the civil rights era "kneel-ins" at historically white churches are also hard to confirm; the Julius Corpening interview is the only one that mentions that there was no attempt made at Watts Street because the church was known to be open.

(I do not discount the importance of these stories. The fact that current members know and repeat them is significant. If this is not exactly who we were, it tells us who we want to be. We have a right to be proud of our history on race relations and that we supported Warren Carr, even if some of the details have become blurry and embellished over the years.)

The oft-told story of Addie Davis's examination for her ordination belongs to Warren Carr, and he told it for many years with relish. It does not belong to Addie Davis. The reference to her private life and supposed virginity screams sexism and the idea of a group of men sitting around deciding a woman's fate partially on the basis of her sex, while accurate, is painful. Her comments that I have included came largely from an article in Notes from Baptist History and Heritage V. 51, issue 1, by Pamela R. Durso.

I also borrowed heavily from 75th-anniversary history written by my father, Warner Ragsdale, and Shirley Strobel, especially for the chapter on Bob McClernon. Shirley was an important member of Watts Street for many years and worked closely with McClernon to establish Threshold. She was a talented, remarkable woman. I miss both my father and Shirley and wish I could have discussed this telling of Watts Street's first 100 years with them.

For more recent things, like the discussion around and development of a welcoming statement, people's memories differ, and I found myself grateful for all the documentation that has survived to be able to put together a timeline. It was an emotional topic discussed over many years, and every story people share is valuable. The difference in what people remember is sometimes surprising.

My thanks to the many who made time to talk with me. And my gratitude to Dorisanne for writing the introduction, to Jim Drennan for the careful editing and additions, and to my intrepid Sunday School class that explored Watts Streets archives during the Sunday School hour, helping me track down exact dates and odds and ends. Above all, thanks to Naomi Nelson, my partner in crime throughout the process. Naomi has found all kinds of books and documents, taken hours to comb through archives, and has listened to more

Watts Street history and tangents I have gone off on than anyone should ever have to. She has been a wonderful editor and friend. Thank you all.

I want to stress that what I have written is *a* history of Watts Street—not *the* history of Watts Street. I have tried to tell the story of Watts Street in the larger world, of a community facing the issues of the times they confronted. I chose to organize this history around the pastoral tenures over these 100 years not because the pastor is the key player but because each pastor seemed to me to represent a different era. The first four pastors, with shorter tenures, seemed together to tell the story of the church's beginning.

The full story of Watts Street is so much richer than the one I have told here, and I would like to encourage everyone to consider writing or recording their own history of the church and depositing it in the archives to enrich this story that belongs to all of us.

Rebecca Ragsdale Lallier

December 2023

1923 Covenant

Having been led, as we believe, by the Spirit of God to receive the Lord Jesus Christ as our Savior; and on the profession of our faith, having been baptized in the name of the Father, and of the Son, and of the Holy Ghost, we do now, the presence of God, angels, and this assembly, most solemnly and joyfully enter into covenant with one another, as one body in Christ.

We engage, therefore, by the aid of the Holy Spirit to walk together in Christian love; to strive for the advancement of this church in knowledge, holiness, and comfort; to promote its prosperity and spirituality; to sustain its worship, ordinances, disciple, and doctrines; to contribute cheerfully and regularly to the support of the ministry, the expenses of the church, the relief of the poor, and the spread of the gospel through all nations, as the Lord has prospered us.

We also engage to maintain family and secret devotions to religiously educate our children to seek the salvation of our kindred and acquaintances, to walk circumspectly in the world; to be just in our dealings, faithful in our engagements, and exemplary in our deportment; and to be zealous in our efforts to advance the kingdom of our Savior.

We further engage to watch over one another in brotherly love; to remember each other in prayer; to aid each other in sickness and distress; to cultivate Christian sympathy and feeling and courtesy in speech; to be slow to take offense but always ready for reconciliation, and mindful of the rules of our Savior, to secure it without delay.

We moreover engage that when we remove from this place, we will, as soon as possible, unite with some other church, where we will carry out the spirit of this covenant and the principles of God's word.

1957 Covenant,
Rev. Warren Carr, Pastor

Since God has called us into covenant with him and has gathered us for his purpose, we, upon a profession of faith, having committed ourselves to Jesus Christ as Savior and Lord, and having been baptized in the name of the Father and of the Son and of the Holy Spirit, do now covenant with one another as one body in Christ:

To God the Father and the Son, under the guidance of the Holy Spirit, we pledge our full obedience and commit ourselves to seek first His kingdom and His righteousness and to honor no persuasion or command contrary to his will.

We covenant to live in this church as disciples, seeking ever to grow in the knowledge of God, and as witnesses to God's redemptive act and sustaining grace. We covenant to attend and support the worship of this church, its ordinances, discipline, and doctrines, to contribute to its support in its total mission by giving of our time, our abilities, and our money.

We covenant to live as Christians in our homes, to engage in family and individual devotions, to teach our children by instruction and example that Christ is Savior and Lord and that in commitment to Him they will find life's highest purpose.

We engage to hold one another in Christian love, to be slow to judge and quick to forgive. We shall not consciously engage in conduct that may cause another to stumble. In compassion, affection, and concern, we shall minister to each other in sickness, distress, and bereavement, pray for each other, be mindful and considerate of one another, and share one another's joys and sorrows.

We further covenant to live as Christians in the world, to be exemplary in our conduct and just in our dealings. We covenant to include all people everywhere within the circle of our love and concern and to regard as of the household of faith all who worship

Christ as Savior and Lord. As we hold to our Baptist heritage, we shall seek with all Christians a unity of spirit and action.

We further resolved that we shall become active members of another church when circumstances require our separation from this one.

In this covenant made, we shall stand firm, holding its principles in sincerity, judging ourselves false to our professed faith if we ignore its demands upon our lives and resources, and renewing it regularly with each other before God in our common worship

1997 Covenant,
Rev. Mel Williams, Pastor

Having been called by God and led by the Holy Spirit to confess Jesus Christ as Lord, and having been baptized into the church gathered in this place and throughout the world, we enter into covenant with God and with one another. We promise:

To worship together, witnessing to God's redemptive and sustaining grace;

To seek to grow in the knowledge of God revealed in Jesus and in our own personal experience;

To study the Bible and to pray for guidance from the Holy Spirit in applying its teachings to our lives;

To instruct others in the Christian faith and in our Baptist heritage;

To teach the children among us by word and example that in obedience to God, they will find life's highest purpose and richest meaning;

To love one another, being slow to judge and quick to forgive;

To celebrate different views and gifts among us, confident that we are one body in Christ;

To minister to one another with compassion, sharing both joys and sorrows;

To contribute time, money, and abilities to the church's ministry; To proclaim the gospel to those who do not know Jesus as savior;

To embody God's forgiveness in all our relationships, both at home and at work;

To promote peace and justice wherever we touch other lives;

To support the mission of the church by feeding, housing, and befriending the needy;

To seek the Kingdom of God on earth, knowing that nothing can separate us from God's love.

We enter this covenant freely, promising to abide by its claims on our lives and to renew it regularly with one another before God.

1988 Church Profile of Watts Street Baptist Church

This profile was created for the pastor search in 1988 which resulted in the hiring of the Rev. Mel Williams.

Watts Street Baptist Church is looking for a pastor. This document describes the church for those pastors who are interested in serving this congregation.

The congregation of Watts Street Baptist Church describes itself as "diverse." Most adult members are college educated and many have professional or graduate degrees. More are over 60 than under 35. A significant number of adult members have grown up in the church. The migration in and out of the Research Triangle makes for a constant but slow turnover among the portion of the congregation not native to Durham. The church's proximity to Duke University and downtown Durham put it in a good position to attract new members from among the people moving to Durham and the Research Triangle, but the church has not been as successful in that effort as most people think it should have been. Many members are conservative, business- oriented people who support the church financially but are not active in the outreach ministry. A significant number (but a minority) are active in the social ministry of the church. They all have in common a tolerance for the different views of other members—on religious doctrine, on the role of the church in society, on politics, etc. Despite its convenient, central location, the church draws members from all parts of Durham County and from portions of Orange and Granville counties. As a result, few of the children active in the church programs have church friends attending the same school.

The quality of the worship experience is of central importance to the congregation. The church has had and expects preaching of high quality. It is a church that believes that the process of becoming a

Christian is a lifelong journey and that the life of Jesus is the surest clue one can find as a guide to that journey. Regular worship services are held twice each morning, but no service is held in the evenings. In worship, music by the adult choir plays an important role. The type of music runs more towards classical sacred music, with limited use of traditional Southern Baptist hymns. Special music services are offered at Sunday worship at Christmas and Easter, and this year, the church has had two worship services consisting almost solely of hymns: one with traditional hymns and the other more classically oriented. Lay leaders commonly participate in the leadership of worship; no distinction between male and female is made in this regard (or in any other). At Christmas, two Moravian love feasts are held and serve as a highlight of the Advent season to many, including many community people not otherwise associated with the church.

The church has a long history of involvement in social ministries. It currently operates a shelter for homeless women and their children—the only such shelter in Durham. It rents portions of its building at a very modest cost to the Durham Nursery School Association for use as a daycare center and to the Dispute Settlement Center for its operations. The group responsible for outreach efforts and mission education, the Board of Missions, is currently implementing an exchange program with citizens of the Soviet Union in an effort to promote a deeper understanding among our congregation of the obstacles to and possibilities for more harmonious relations between the two countries. In addition to those current programs, the church has in the past been instrumental in organizing the Host Homes program at Duke Hospital (it provides rooms and private homes at little or no cost for families of patients at Duke Hospital) and the Meals on Wheels program. Both those programs are now run by Durham Congregations In Action, an ecumenical social ministries organization in which the church is active and in which its members volunteer frequently. The president and two key committee chairmen of the Durham Habitat for Humanity affiliate are church members, and the affiliate began as a result of the efforts of church members. Other past mission involvements include the provision of financial support and nursing care for migrants and the sponsorship of families from Poland and

Cambodia who immigrated to Durham. Finally, church members are active in other local programs such as the Community Soup Kitchen and Threshold, a support group and clubhouse for chronically mentally ill adults. The Board of Mission also supports most of these (as well as national and international) programs financially. That financial support is not unusual. The unusual thing about the church is the extent to which a small but significant minority of its members actively give of their time for such projects and the ability they have to conceive an idea and actually implement it.

The educational program of the church includes a traditional Sunday morning church school. It also provides Sunday evening programs and retreats for middle school and senior high youth. Special programs such as intergenerational programs, a January bible study comma and summer Sunday school forums on specific topics such as hunger or peace are also offered regularly.

Governance of the church is typically Baptist. The congregation makes all significant decisions based on recommendations of the major Boards and Committees of the church. The congregation meets regularly three times a year on Sunday evenings. The Board of Deacons acts as the "Board of Directors," although that system of governance is under review by the congregation. Women have served as deacons since the mid-1960s and now comprise about half the membership on the Board. The Board is also responsible for the spiritual life of the church. To that end, it has subcommittees dealing with Fellowship, New Members and Good News, and Lay Pastoral Care. The subcommittees are active, but the time required of the Board to accomplish its administrative duties and the more difficult nature of the spiritual duties make it difficult for them to adequately accomplish their purposes. A promising development in this area, however, is the establishment of a Stephen Ministry in the congregation in 1987; the first class of Stephens Ministers is in training, and the congregation is expectantly awaiting the day they will graduate.

The church is a member of the North Carolina Baptist and Southern Baptist Conventions, as well as the American Baptist Churches of the USA. It has a fraternal relationship with the Church of the Brethren. In some of these denominal relationships, the church is experiencing a time of turbulence. It is not the first time. In the late 1960s the church adopted a policy that allows persons to transfer membership from other churches, even if they have not been baptized by immersion. As a result of that and other policies, the church's standing in the local Baptist Association was questioned by both the church and the Association. To this day the church's relationship with the Association is strained. In recent years, the trend toward extremist leadership at the Southern Baptist Convention has prompted the congregation to withhold funds on two occasions. In addition, it sent delegates to national conventions on several occasions in an effort to elect a more moderate slate of leaders for the convention. The church's future policy towards the convention awaits further developments at the national level.

The church staff has a tradition of stability. The last two senior pastors have served for 22 and 18 years. The other staff consists of a full-time Minister of Education (9 years experience at the church), a part-time minister of music (30 hours per week, 15 plus years of experience), and a full-time secretary (5 years experience). Custodial services are contracted for, and the Minister of Music receives a small stipend to serve as the building manager. During the academic year, the church has a student intern from Southeastern or Duke Divinity School and occasionally has an additional intern from Germany through Duke.

The church building is a striking stone structure that is three stories high, with lovely stained-glass windows on three sides of the sanctuary. It is 64 years old but is currently in a good repair period. No major capital replacements seem to be needed at this time. The sanctuary and classrooms are adequate to accommodate significant growth without further physical expansion.

In the last two years, the church has completed an extensive long- term planning process. In addition, the membership was surveyed this fall in an effort to make the production of this profile as accurate as possible. The results of both indicate that the congregation is seeking to nurture the spiritual growth of its membership, become more caring towards each other, increase its membership, and improve its Christian education program.

The Watts Street Baptist Church is made up of: People (diverse but talented and committed); A strong worship tradition; An outreach program that is without equality in the city; An experienced staff; An elegant building; And much more. It is a church seeking leadership to help it continue on its journey towards becoming Christian.

Do Justice, Love Kindness, Walk Humbly

Charter Members

J. M. Airheart

Mrs. J. M. Airheart

Miss Georgia Airheart

Milton Airheart

B. D. Aslin

Mrs. B. D. Aslin

Miss Maude Baity

H. C. Barbee

Mrs. II. C. Barbee

Mrs. O. D. Barbee

Mrs. L. H. Barbour

Mrs. Mary Beavers

Wesley F. Beavers

S. B. Black

Mrs. S. B. Black

J. T. Blackman

Mrs. J. T. Blackman

E. H. Bowling

Mrs. E. H. Bowling

Edwin Bowling

J. E. Bowling

Mrs. J. E. Bowling

J. M. Bowling

J. W. Bright

Courtney Bright

Miss Dorothy Bright

Miss Ruth Bright

W. L. Brown

Mrs. W. L. Brown

Miss Lucille Bullard

S. A. Carter

Mrs. S. A. Carter

W. C. Carter

Mrs. W. C. Carter

Miss Eunice Chaplin

Miss Bennie Cheek

J. M. Cheek

Mrs. J. M. Cheek

F. R. Clark

Mrs. F. R. Clark

Miss Esther Crutchfield

W. H. Crutchfield

Mrs. W. H. Crutchfield

Miss Florence Crutchfield

Fred Colclough

Mrs. Fred Colclough

M. O. Cole

Mrs. M. O. Cole

Miss Coma Cole

Philip Cole

W. J. H. Cotton

Mrs. W. J. H. Cotton

R. L. Deas

Mrs. R. L. Deas

I.S. Eubanks

B. W. Fassett

Mrs. B. W. Fassett

B. T. Hicks

Mrs. B. T. Hicks

Otis High

Miss Leona Hinton

J. L. Horne

E. Clyde Johnson

Mrs. E. Clyde Johnson

L. W. Jones

Mrs. L. W. Jones

R. M. Kinton

Mrs. R. M. Kinton

Mrs. J. L. Kirkland

Jack Kirkland

C. B. Laws

Mrs. C. B. Laws

Mrs. Bessie Lowe

W. Aubyn Lyon

Mrs. W. Aubyn Lyon

W. C. Lyon

Mrs. W. C. Lyon

Frederick Lyon

Miss Margaret Lyon

Wortham Lyon

Mrs. R. W. Malone

D.C. May

Mrs. D. C. May

Miss Elise May

Miss Julia May

D.S. Miller Jr.

Miss Evelyn Miller

Luther C. Morris

J.T. Salmon

Mrs. J. T. Salmon

Mrs. Luther C. Morris

Mrs. C. J. Muse

Hendricks Muse

J. W. Muse

Marvin H. Muse

Mrs. J.W. Neal

C.P. Norris

Mrs. C.P. Norris

Miss Mary Norris

Mrs. T. L. Pace

Miss Dora Page

Miss Mamie Page

Mrs. W. G. Parrish

E.C. Piper

Mrs. E. C. Piper

Mrs. Julia Poole

H.M. Reams

Mrs. H. M. Reams

Miss Helen Reams

Mrs. B.T. Roberts, Sr.

Miss Ruth Rogers

Miss Evelyn Salmon

Thomas Salmon

W. A. Salmon

I.W Satterwhite

Mrs. I W. Satterwhite

Miss Margaret Satterwhite

Mrs. Charles Scarlette

E.G. Shaw

Mrs. E.G. Shaw

R. J. Shaw

Mrs. R. J. Shaw

C. H. Shipp

Miss Elsie Shipp

Miss Helen Shipp

Miss Mary Shipp

Mrs. S. N. Slade Norman Slade

Miss Felicia Slade

Mrs. Viola Suit John Sweaney

Mrs. John Sweaney

Miss Lois Sweaney

Mrs. O. V. Thomspon

W.C. Timberlake

Mrs. W. C. Timberlake

E. C. Tilley

E.G. Tilley

Miss Pauline Tilley

Mrs. Wallace Tuck

Mrs. Walter Warren

C.W. Weathington

Mrs. C. W. Weathington

Mrs. J. W. Wilkerson,

Sr. Louis Wilkerson

O. F. Williams

Mrs. O. F. Williams

W. H. Young

Mrs. W. H. Young

ClaiborneYoungMiss Foye Young

Miss Margaret Young

Victor Young

William Young

Mr. and Mrs. A. J. Draughon added in 1998

Watts Street Ministers

Pastors, Music Staff, and Ministerial Interns at Watts Street Baptist Church

Senior Pastors

Howard Weeks, 1923 to 1925

Sylvester Green, 1926 to 1932

J.T. Riddick, 1932 to 1938

Owen Herring, 1929 to 1946

Warren Carr, 1946 to 1964

Robert McClernon, 1965 to 1987

Mel Williams, 1988 to 2012

Dorisanne Cooper, 2014 to present

Ministers of Education

Jean Dula (Fletcher), 1955 to 1958

John Long, 1958 to 1962

John Davis, 1963 to 1967

Carol Fox, 1966 to 1967

Jim Grant, 1967 to 1973

Hugh Dukes, 1973 to 1976

Wallace Kuroiwa, 1977 to 1978

Judy Berry and Beth Crisp, 1978 to 1979

Dick Chorley, 1979 to 2002

Minister to Adults

Diane Eubanks Hill, 2003 to 2018

Minister with Children and Their Families

Diane Eubanks Hill, 1992 to 2003

Esther Soud Parker, 2013 to 2022

Ministers with Children, Youth and Their Families

Kelly Sasser, 2003 to 2011

Minister with Youth and Their Families

Kelly Sasser, 2011 to 2022

Interim Director of Children's Ministries

Kacey Reynolds Schedler 2011 to 2012

Minister with Children and Congregational Life

Esther Soud Parker, 2022 to present

Minister with Youth and Community Life

Kelly Sasser, 2022 to present

Music Ministers and Organists

Director of Music Ministry unless otherwise noted

Judith Eckerman 1956 to 1959

Julie Bonnet 1959 to 1961

Stephen Sigler 1961 to 1963

Richard Joiner 1964 to 1968

William Treichler 1969

Richard Joiner 1969 to 1970

Kenneth Harrell 1970 to 1997

Larry Speakman, 1998 to 2012

Melody Zentner, 2012 to present (interim until 2017)

Tom Bloom, Organist 1998 to present

Children's and Youth Choir Coordinators

Mary Elizabeth Hanchey, Children's Choir Director and Coordinator, 2012 to 2018

Jonathan Emmons, Interim Youth Choir Director, 2014

Troy Pickens, Interim Youth Choir Director, 2015-2017

Cara Valenti, Children's and Youth Choir Coordinator, 2017 to present

Ministerial Interns

Charles Smith, 1965 to 1966

Paul Clark, 1966 to 1967

Jack Clifford, 1967 to 1968

Robert McKeowan, 1971 to 1972

Hugh Dukes, 1972 to 1973

Cathy Blythewood, 1979 to 1980

Beth Graham, 1980

David Stricklin, 1981 to 1982

Joseph Flair, 1982 to 1983

Andrea O'Connell, 1983 to 1984

Gayle Strikeleather, 1985 to 1986

Karen Isaman, 1987 to 1989

Renee Collins, 1989 Summer only

Courtney Kruger, 1989 to 1991

Stan Wilson, 1991 to 1993

Beth Toler, 1993 to 1995

Mark Anthony Middleton, 1995 fall semester only

Lee Canipe, 1996 to 1998

Matt Norvell, 1999 to 2001

Kacey Reynolds, 2001 to 2003

Mary Elizabeth Hanchey, 2015 to 2016

Claire Dillashaw, 2022 to 2023

Watts Street Ordinands

C. Sylvester Green	1926
T. Rupert Coleman	1928
James Cansler	1950
Max Wicker	1952
John Stone	1960
Addie Davis	1964
Charles Smith	1968
Paul Clark, Jr.	1968
Allen F. Page	1968
William M. Hall	1970
Roland Johnson	1971
John Rogers	1973
Gilbert Fauber	1973
Bryant Kendrick	1973
Lisa Grabarek Matthews	1974
Phil Motley	1976
Nancy Stanton	1977
Al Bell	1978
Andrea O'Connell	1986
Danny Green	1986

Paul Boone	1987
Clay Berry	1987
Carol Jackson Cothran	1989
Courtney Kruger	1992
LaDayne McCleese Polaski	1993
Stan Wilson	1994
Beth Toler	1998
Matt Norvell	2001
José Luis Villaseñor	2008
Christine Peterman	2008
Rob Womack	2013
Kathy Turner	2013
Matt Dodrill	2015
Kevin Georgas	2015
Russ Ames	2016
Mary Elizabeth Hanchey	2017
Amy Armstrong	2018
Abby Post	2021

www.ingramcontent.com/pod-product-compliance
Lightning Source LLC
Chambersburg PA
CBHW051156120626
46547CB00012B/1092